HOW THINGS WORK

MONSTER MACHINES

Peter Lafferty

DP

DEMPSEY
PARR

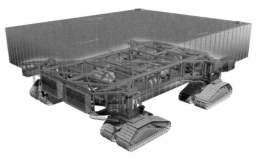

This is a Dempsey Parr Book
This edition published in 2000
Dempsey Parr is an imprint of Parragon

Parragon
Queen Street House
4 Queen Street
Bath BA1 1HE, UK

Copyright © Parragon 2000

All rights reserved. No part of this publication may be
reproduced, stored in a retrieval system or transmitted,
in any form or by any means, electronic, mechanical,
photocopying, recording or otherwise, without the
prior permission of the copyright holders.

ISBN 1-84084-855-3

Printed in Dubai, U.A.E.

Produced by
Monkey Puzzle Media Ltd
Gissing's Farm
Fressingfield
Suffolk IP21 5SH
UK

Illustrations: Alex Pang, Cara Kong,
Adrian Wright and Studio Liddell
Designer: Tim Mayer
Cover design: Victoria Webb
Editor: Linda Sonntag
Editorial assistance: Lynda Lines and Jenny Siklós
Indexer: Caroline Hamilton
Project manager: Katie Orchard

Photos supplied by MPM Images

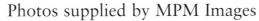

Contents

GIANT MACHINES

The machines in this book are monster-sized.
They are the biggest machines around. The book
is arranged so that you can take in these gigantic
monsters at a glance. While you are looking at them,
try to imagine the noise and the smell that they make
and the thrill of standing next to them.

A HELPING HAND

All machines do something useful. Some machines
do jobs that need enormous power. A crane lifts huge
loads, multiplying the puny strength of a human
being many times. A flood barrier holds back
the tide. A nuclear power station splits atoms.
A turbogenerator produces electricity by moving
a magnet near a coil of wire. A person can make
electricity in this way, but only when the process is
scaled up to monster size—and a giant machine takes
over—is a useful amount of electricity produced.

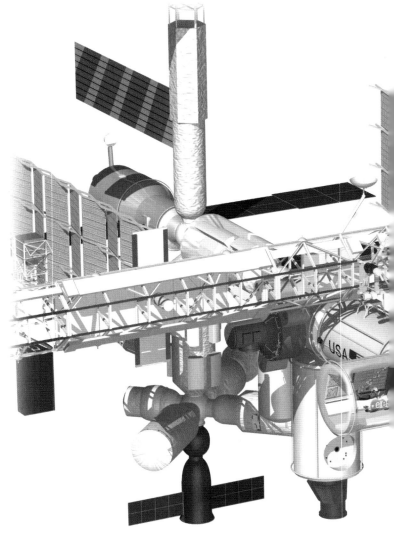

Space station
A space station (above) is a machine
for astronauts to live in while they
are in orbit above the Earth.

ROBOT WORKERS
Industrial robots help to manufacture cars. In some
ways, they are perfect workers—they never get tired,
sick, or bored, and they don't need vacations!

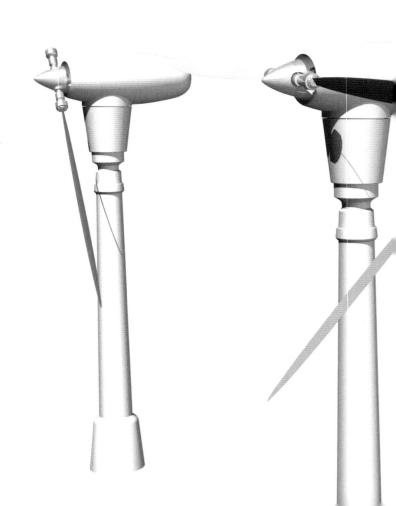

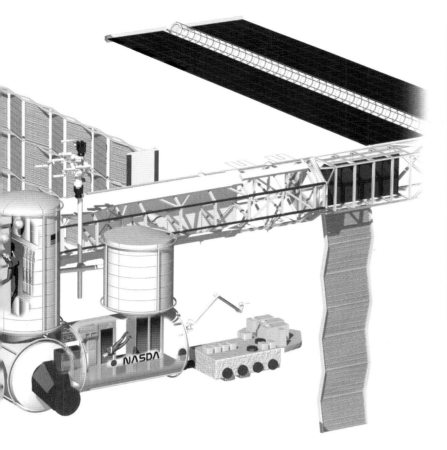

MOVABLE TYPE
Printers used to make print using individual letters, carved into small wooden blocks. The blocks were placed in a frame, wiped with ink, and pressed onto paper to produce the printed page. This process is called letterpress printing. Today, huge machines have taken over the job.

VERY ACCURATE
Monster machines may be powerful, but they are also designed for accuracy. An industrial robot can weld together the metal parts of a car body for hour after hour without getting tired, and without making any mistakes that might make the car unsafe on the road. A radio telescope looks deep into outer space and detects objects much too far away to be seen by the naked eye. A flight simulator mimics the behavior of an airplane so well that a trainee pilot can't tell the difference between flying the simulator and the real thing.

JUST FOR FUN
Some monster machines have been designed just for fun. A roller coaster makes riders sick with delight as they hurtle down stomach-churning drops. A Ferris wheel lifts its passengers high in the sky for a bird's-eye view of the world.

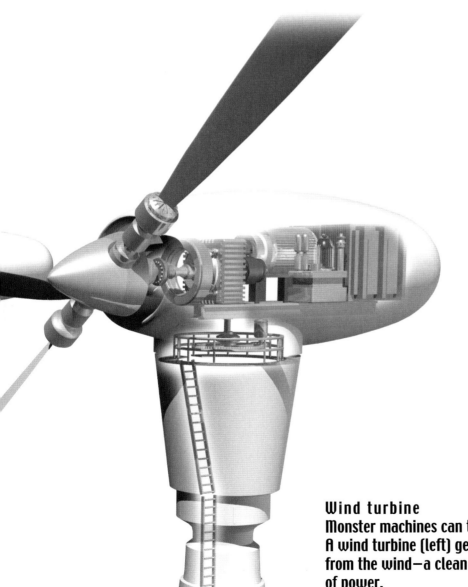

Wind turbine
Monster machines can take us into the future. A wind turbine (left) generates electrical energy from the wind—a clean and renewable source of power.

DREDGER

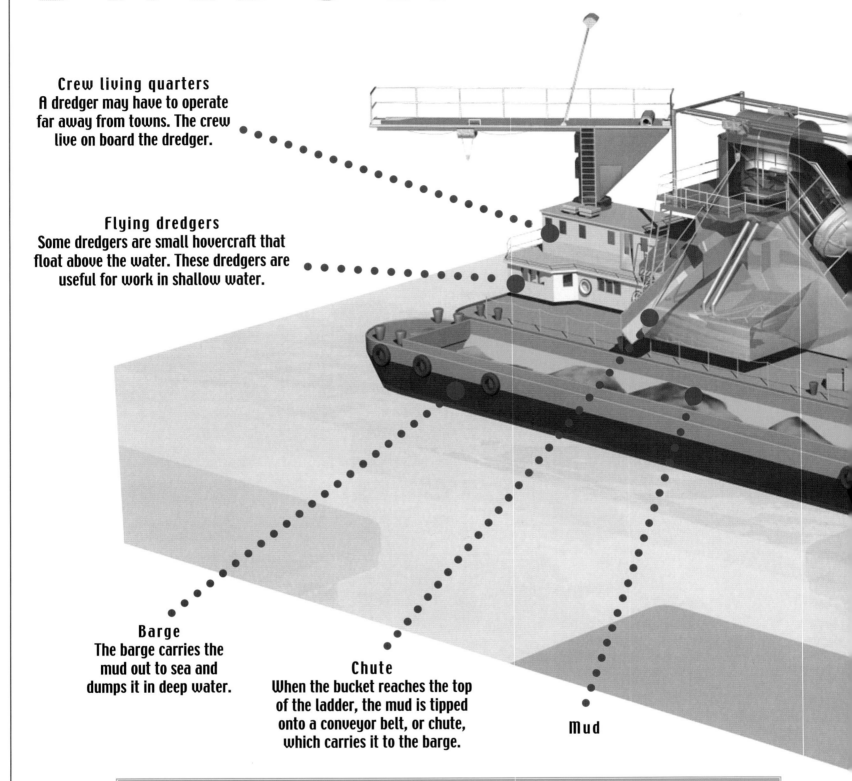

Crew living quarters
A dredger may have to operate far away from towns. The crew live on board the dredger.

Flying dredgers
Some dredgers are small hovercraft that float above the water. These dredgers are useful for work in shallow water.

Barge
The barge carries the mud out to sea and dumps it in deep water.

Chute
When the bucket reaches the top of the ladder, the mud is tipped onto a conveyor belt, or chute, which carries it to the barge.

Mud

THE SHIP THAT DIGS

A dredger is a special ship that clears harbors and rivers by digging up mud or rocks from the seabed, or riverbed, that might get in the way of passing ships. Dredgers are used for clearing out and deepening harbors, rivers, and canals. They are also used to remove the silt—soft, fine mud—that settles on harbor bottoms, riverbeds, and canalbeds. There are many different kinds of dredgers, but they all have a mechanism that dredges unwanted material from the bottoms of waterways. The soil, silt, or rock is then carried to the surface and tipped out onto a barge, which carries it away for disposal. Dredgers can work at depths of up to 160ft (50m).

Crane

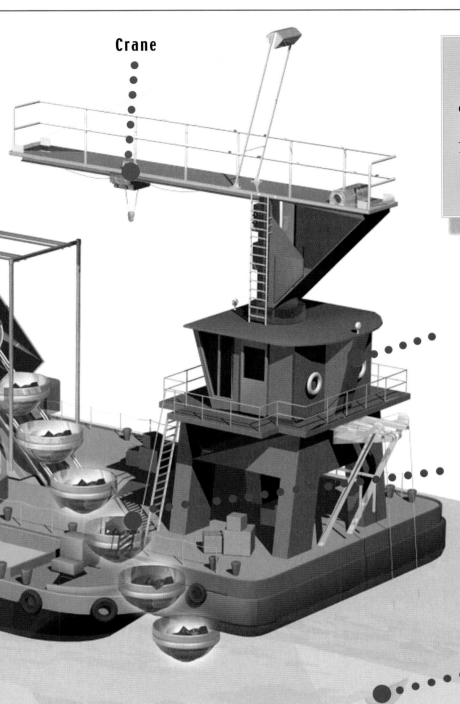

POWERFUL MACHINE
The world's most powerful dredger is called *Prins der Nederlanden*. It can lift 19,680 tons of mud from a depth of 115ft (35m) in less than an hour. It uses two suction tubes to lift the mud.

Control deck
The dredger captain lowers the ladder to the seabed, and controls the speed of the buckets.

Buckets
The chain of buckets is called a ladder. Each bucket is shaped like a scoop. The buckets scoop up the mud from the river bottom or seabed.

Deep dredging
Bucket dredgers can work in water as deep as 160ft (50m).

Looking for minerals
Dredgers are sometimes used to mine the seabed. In this case, the material lifted from the seabed is not dumped, but taken by barge to a refinery where useful minerals are extracted from it.

ALL SHAPES AND SIZES
The bucket dredger is the most common kind of dredger. This has a continuous chain of buckets reaching down on a ladder to the seabed. The buckets go around on the chain like the stairs on an escalator. At the bottom, the buckets dig into the seabed. They come up to the surface carrying mud and dump it when they reach the top of the chain. A suction dredger is often used for dredging silt. It vacuums up the silt through a suction pipe. Some dredgers use a mechanical arm with a scoop that scrapes material from the seabed. Other dredgers use an auger to lift material from the bottom. An auger is like a large corkscrew inside a cylinder. As the screw turns, it lifts material up the tube.

BUCKETWHEEL EXCAVATOR

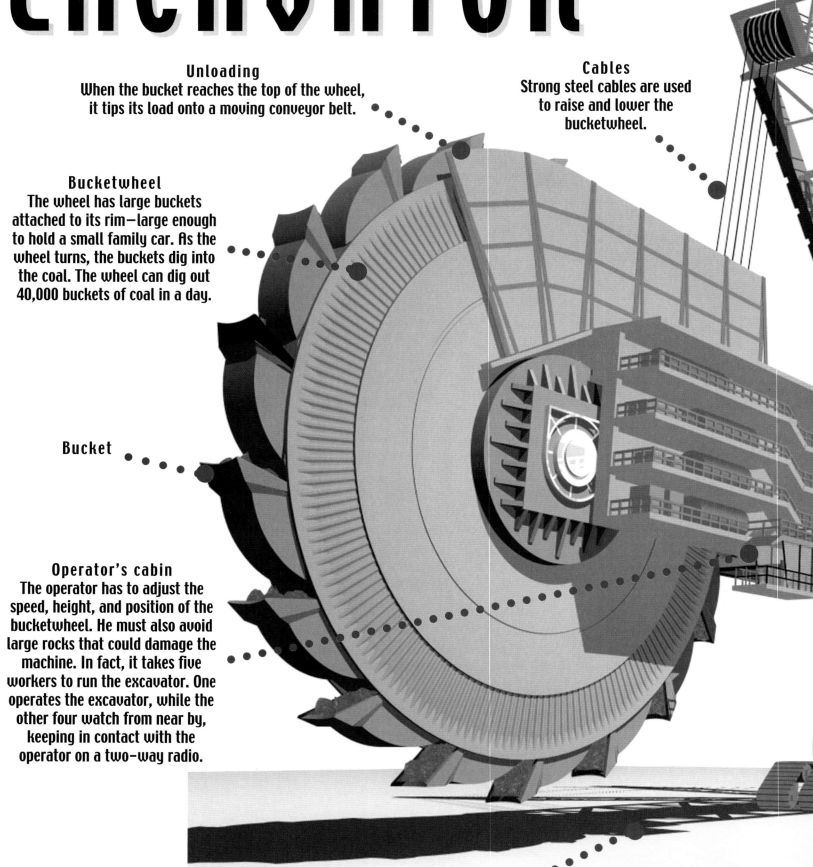

Unloading
When the bucket reaches the top of the wheel, it tips its load onto a moving conveyor belt.

Cables
Strong steel cables are used to raise and lower the bucketwheel.

Bucketwheel
The wheel has large buckets attached to its rim—large enough to hold a small family car. As the wheel turns, the buckets dig into the coal. The wheel can dig out 40,000 buckets of coal in a day.

Bucket

Operator's cabin
The operator has to adjust the speed, height, and position of the bucketwheel. He must also avoid large rocks that could damage the machine. In fact, it takes five workers to run the excavator. One operates the excavator, while the other four watch from near by, keeping in contact with the operator on a two-way radio.

Strip mine
A large mine, such as the copper strip mine at Bingham Canyon, near Salt Lake City, Utah, can produce 265,680 tons of ore in a day. The deepest strip mine in the world is near Bergheim, Germany. It is 1,066ft (325m) deep.

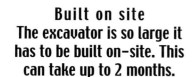

MONSTER MINING MACHINE

The gigantic bucketwheel excavator is a powerful machine used in strip mining, where the coal is just under the surface of the ground. First the soil on top of the coal is scraped away. Then the excavator digs the coal with its huge buckets, which turn on a revolving belt. It dumps the coal onto a conveyor belt that carries it off to be stored, or to waiting railroad trucks. Bucketwheel excavators are also used in quarries to mine minerals and metal ores. For these jobs, the machine is fitted with a crusher. First the rock is blasted, then the excavator scoops it up, crushes it, and feeds it onto the conveyor belts.

Built on site
The excavator is so large it has to be built on-site. This can take up to 2 months.

Boom
The boom, or frame, supports the wheel and conveyor belt.

Engines
Powerful diesel engines are needed to turn the bucketwheel.

Crusher
The huge lumps of coal or ore may pass through a crusher inside the machine. This grinds them to a size that's easier to handle.

Conveyor belt
A conveyor belt carries the coal to a railroad siding where it is dumped into a railroad truck. Some coal may be piled up in a storage area.

Crawler tracks
The excavator moves on huge crawler tracks. Each track is larger than a semi. This machine has 16 tracks.

GUIDED BY LASER

It may be a monster machine, but the bucketwheel excavator is also a precision instrument that uses the very latest laser technology. A laser beam guides the excavator on its path so that its buckets cut into the coal face at exactly the right place and to the right depth. If the excavator is not in exactly the right place, it will dig out rock and soil as well as coal, making the operation less efficient and more expensive. The bucketwheel excavator was one of the first industrial machines to be equipped with a laser.

CONCRETE MIXER TRUCK

Drum
Just before the truck arrives at the construction site, the driver pumps water into the drum. The drum turns about 12 times a minute to mix the concrete.

Hopper
Sand, cement dust, and crushed rock are loaded into the drum through the hopper.

Mixing blades
Welded inside the drum are spiral-shaped blades called flights. These push the concrete to the front or back of the drum, depending on which way the drum is turning.

Unloading
To unload the concrete, the driver changes the direction of the drum. The concrete pours out of the drum onto the delivery chute.

Delivery chute
Concrete pours down the delivery chute to the concrete pump.

Delivery pipe
The concrete is pumped through a pipe on the outside of the boom. The pipe is made in sections that pass through the boom at the joints. This allows the pipe and boom to be folded for storage.

Swivel
This turns to point the boom in the correct direction so that the concrete goes where it is needed.

POURING CONCRETE
Concrete is pumped to the upper stories of a tall building. The hopper delivering the concrete can move to allow the concrete to be spread wherever it is needed.

MIXING CONCRETE

Concrete is used to build tall blocks of offices and apartments cheaply and quickly. It is a wet mixture of sand, cement, crushed rock, and water that sets hard as it dries. When an office block is being built, wet concrete is poured into a steel framework, where it dries to form the floors and walls of the building. Concrete is made and delivered to the building site in a concrete mixer truck. The truck has a large revolving drum to hold the dry ingredients and the driver pumps in water just before the truck reaches the site. The drum turns all the time to keep the concrete well-mixed and to keep it from setting. The truck holds about 15 tons of concrete. It is over 24ft (7m) long and weighs just under 6 tons when unloaded.

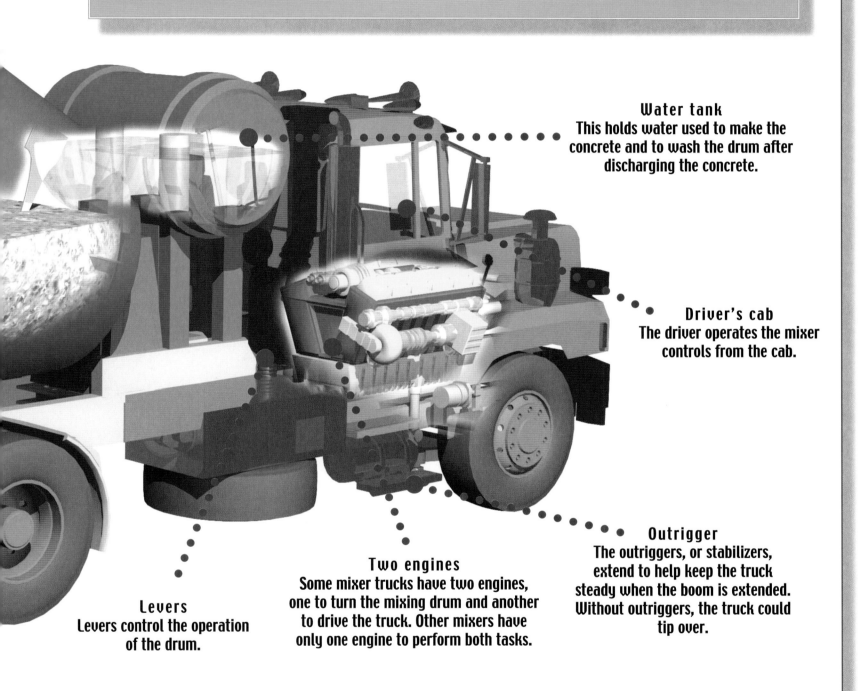

Water tank
This holds water used to make the concrete and to wash the drum after discharging the concrete.

Driver's cab
The driver operates the mixer controls from the cab.

Outrigger
The outriggers, or stabilizers, extend to help keep the truck steady when the boom is extended. Without outriggers, the truck could tip over.

Two engines
Some mixer trucks have two engines, one to turn the mixing drum and another to drive the truck. Other mixers have only one engine to perform both tasks.

Levers
Levers control the operation of the drum.

PUMPING CONCRETE

The mixer truck arrives at the construction site and the driver unloads the concrete by reversing the direction of the mixing drum. The concrete flows down the delivery chute into a concrete pump. A piston in the pump forces the wet concrete through a long pipe and into the building. The machine has to be extremely powerful to pump concrete into the upper stories. Workers smooth the concrete over the floor, or channel it into hollow casings to form the walls. When the concrete sets hard, the casing is removed.

EARTHSCRAPER

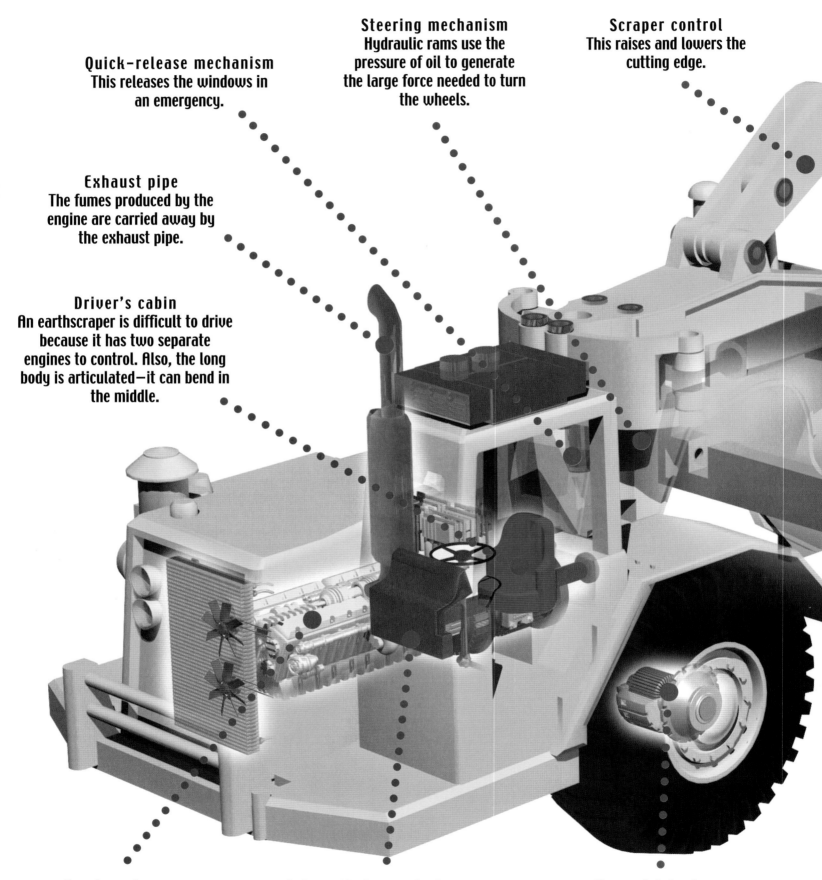

Quick-release mechanism
This releases the windows in an emergency.

Steering mechanism
Hydraulic rams use the pressure of oil to generate the large force needed to turn the wheels.

Scraper control
This raises and lowers the cutting edge.

Exhaust pipe
The fumes produced by the engine are carried away by the exhaust pipe.

Driver's cabin
An earthscraper is difficult to drive because it has two separate engines to control. Also, the long body is articulated—it can bend in the middle.

Front engine
The front engine is a powerful four-stroke diesel engine with 16 cylinders, like a large truck engine.

Automatic transmission
The transmission automatically adjusts the amount of power fed to the wheels from the engine. Less power is needed in loose soils than in hard, compacted soils.

Powerful brakes
The earthscraper has powerful brakes. These work by pressing a pad called a brake shoe against a drum attached to each wheel.

SMOOTHING THE GROUND

An earthscraper is a huge machine used to level and smooth out large areas of ground. This machine is 49ft (15m) long and 11ft (3.4m) wide. It weighs 86 tons—as much as 60 family cars. Road construction teams use earthscrapers to cut through low hills so that a new road can be laid. The machine stores the soil it scrapes away. It can either dump it in one place to build up an embankment, or release it gradually, spreading it over the ground to fill in small pockets in the ground.

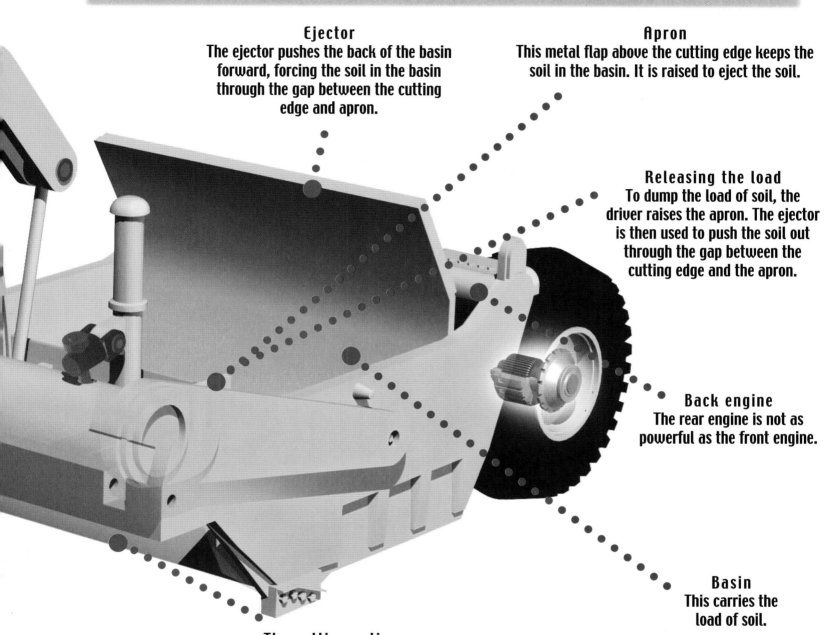

Ejector
The ejector pushes the back of the basin forward, forcing the soil in the basin through the gap between the cutting edge and apron.

Apron
This metal flap above the cutting edge keeps the soil in the basin. It is raised to eject the soil.

Releasing the load
To dump the load of soil, the driver raises the apron. The ejector is then used to push the soil out through the gap between the cutting edge and the apron.

Back engine
The rear engine is not as powerful as the front engine.

Basin
This carries the load of soil.

The cutting action
The cutting edge cuts 12in (300mm) into the ground. After it is lowered, the cutter slices easily through the ground—the soil curls up like butter on a knife. The soil moves into the basin where it is stored until dumping.

WORKING IN PAIRS

An earthscraper has two engines. One powers the front of the machine, where the driver sits, and the other powers the back, where the scraper cutting edge is. Two earthscrapers are often teamed up so a job can be done twice as fast. Double earthscrapers often get stuck in soft ground. A bulldozer has to push them out. The back of the scraper is specially strengthened to handle the force of the bulldozer.

POWER SHOVEL

Small shovel
This power shovel is a small one. It is only 43ft (13m) long and weighs just under 6 tons.

Boom

Open and shut
This ram uses oil pressure to transmit the force of a piston to the bucket bottom. This system, called a hydraulic ram, opens and closes the bucket.

Up and down
This hydraulic ram raises and lowers the boom.

Bucket
The bucket is hinged in the middle so it can open to drop a load. Some very big mining shovels have eight buckets attached to a large wheel that revolves as the machine cuts into the coal.

Replaceable teeth
The teeth on the bucket are designed to sharpen themselves as they cut into the coal. They can be replaced when they eventually wear out.

Headlight
Powerful headlights shine on the coal for working at night.

Swing motor
The swing table is turned by an electric or hydraulic motor. This swings the boom around for unloading.

Bucket hinge
The bucket opens and shuts here.

COMPUTER CONTROLS

Monster machines like the power shovel need to be carefully controlled, or they could do a lot of damage. If they are overloaded or break down they are extremely expensive to repair. So the power shovel has built-in computer systems that automatically shut down the engine if there is the danger of being overloaded. Sensors around the shovel monitor engine performance, temperature, and oil pressure. The computer gives a warning if the engine is not operating correctly.

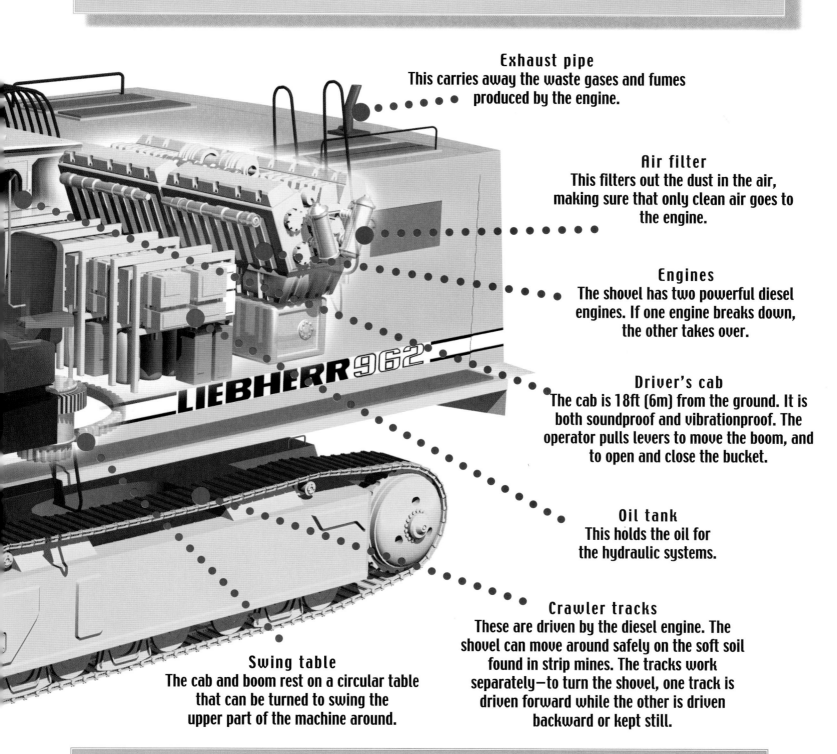

Exhaust pipe
This carries away the waste gases and fumes produced by the engine.

Air filter
This filters out the dust in the air, making sure that only clean air goes to the engine.

Engines
The shovel has two powerful diesel engines. If one engine breaks down, the other takes over.

Driver's cab
The cab is 18ft (6m) from the ground. It is both soundproof and vibrationproof. The operator pulls levers to move the boom, and to open and close the bucket.

Oil tank
This holds the oil for the hydraulic systems.

Crawler tracks
These are driven by the diesel engine. The shovel can move around safely on the soft soil found in strip mines. The tracks work separately—to turn the shovel, one track is driven forward while the other is driven backward or kept still.

Swing table
The cab and boom rest on a circular table that can be turned to swing the upper part of the machine around.

BIG DIGGER

A power shovel digs coal out of the walls of an coal strip mine. This monster machine has a huge bucket at the end of a long arm, or boom—it carries up to 1,507cu ft (140cu m) of coal. The boom stretches up the mine to scrape out coal with the bucket. When the bucket is full, the driver swings the arm around and dumps the coal onto a waiting semi. A power shovel works fast—it can fill a large semi with 118 tons of coal in just two minutes. Power shovels are driven by gasoline or diesel engines, or by electric motors.

The Marion 6360 power shovel has a boom length of 220ft (67m) and a reach of 236ft (72m). It weighs 1,082 tons, and uses 20 electric motors to power the boom and bucket. It works in a strip mine near Percy, Illinois.

TUNNEL BORING MACHINE

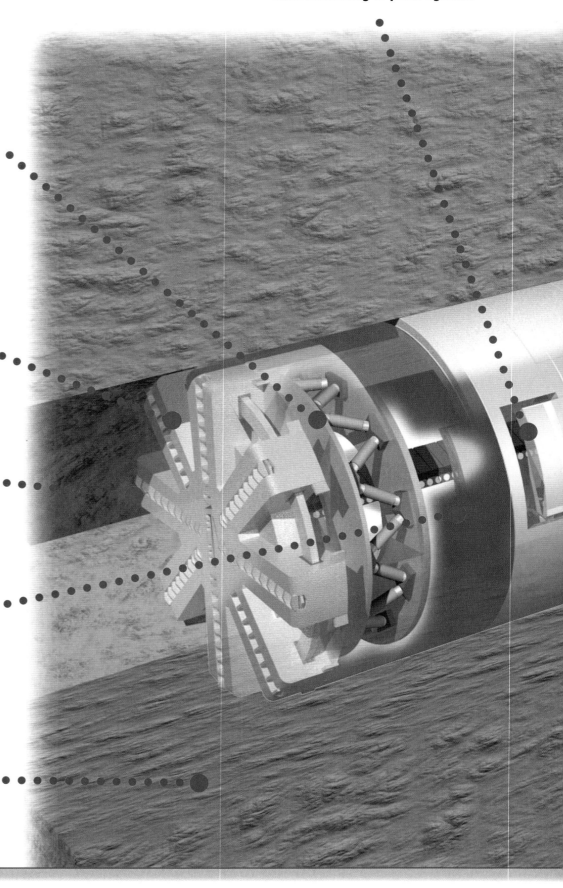

Gripper ram
The hydraulic rams in the gripper section press hard against the tunnel lining, so that the main thrusting rams have something to press against.

Main thrusting rams
These powerful hydraulic rams push the cutting head forward. They work in the same way as the hydraulic lifting arm of an excavator. The force of a piston is transferred by a liquid (usually oil) to where it is needed. Hydraulic systems magnify the force of the piston and can shift heavy loads.

Cutting head
The circular cutting head turns between 2–4 times every minute. Its sharp teeth scrape away rock and soil, which is carried away on a conveyor belt.

Cutting teeth

Telescopic metal skin
This extends between the cutting head and the concrete lining. As the TBM moves forward, the skin extends to cover the gap between the TBM and the concrete tunnel lining.

Soft ground
The ground under water is usually soft and easy to cut through with a TBM. Special cutting heads are used to tunnel through hard rocks.

THE LONGEST TUNNELS

The world's longest tunnel is a water supply tunnel 105mi (169km) long that runs to New York City. The longest rail tunnel is the Seikan Tunnel between the islands of Honshu and Hokkaido in Japan. It has an overall length of 33mi (54km), with a 14mi (23km) underwater section. The Channel Tunnel between England and France is the longest underwater tunnel. It runs under the English Channel for 23mi (38km).

Road and rail tunnels are cut by giant machines that burrow through the ground. The biggest of these machines are called tunnel boring machines (TBMs). The TBMs used to build the Channel Tunnel were 28ft (9m) in diameter and weighed 1,550 tons. With a service train connected behind it, the TBM was 853ft (260m) long—longer than two football fields laid end to end.
These TBMs could travel through soft rock at a speed of only about 0.62mi (1km) per month.

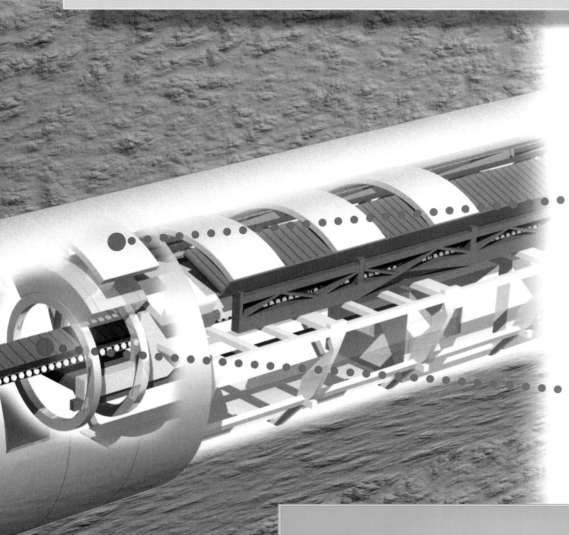

Lining segment
As the cutter moves forward, concrete lining segments are placed around the tunnel wall. These seal the tunnel and keep water from getting in. As each lining segment is installed, the gripper section is moved forward to catch up with the cutting head.

Conveyor belt
This carries away the rocks.

BURROWING MACHINES

A TBM is like a long metal tube. At the front, the cutting head cuts through rock with huge rotating blades. Inside the tube, there are hydraulic rams that move the machine forward, conveyor belts to carry away the broken rock, and a control cabin.

TOWER CRANE

ANCHOR

The tower is anchored to large concrete blocks or set into a concrete base. Above 200ft (60m), a tower crane is often linked to the building it is working on for extra stability.

Lifting winch
This winch winds in the hoist cables to lift the load. The rope is wound around a drum. The winch is powered by an electric motor.

Trolley winch
This winch winds in the cables attached to the trolley to move it along the main jib.

Counterweight jib
This long arm, or jib, carries the counterweights.

Driver's cab
The driver sits in a cab and controls the winches that move the trolley along the arm and lift the load. A worker on the ground guides the driver using a walkie-talkie radio. An alarm system in the cab warns the driver if a load is too heavy to lift.

Counterweights
These heavy concrete blocks balance the crane and keep it from falling over as it lifts a load.

Tower
The tower is made up of steel sections bolted together. Each section is 20ft (6m) tall.

Ladder
The driver may have to climb over 100 steps to reach the cab.

GOING UP

Tower cranes are built piece by piece on the construction site. They get slowly taller as more sections are added to the tower. A small mobile crane places the first few sections of the tower in place. After that, a special section, called a climbing frame, is added. The crane lifts a new section and places it inside the climbing frame. A hydraulic ram, a lifting device at the base of the climbing frame, pushes the new section up. The climbing frame is then raised and the whole process is repeated again.

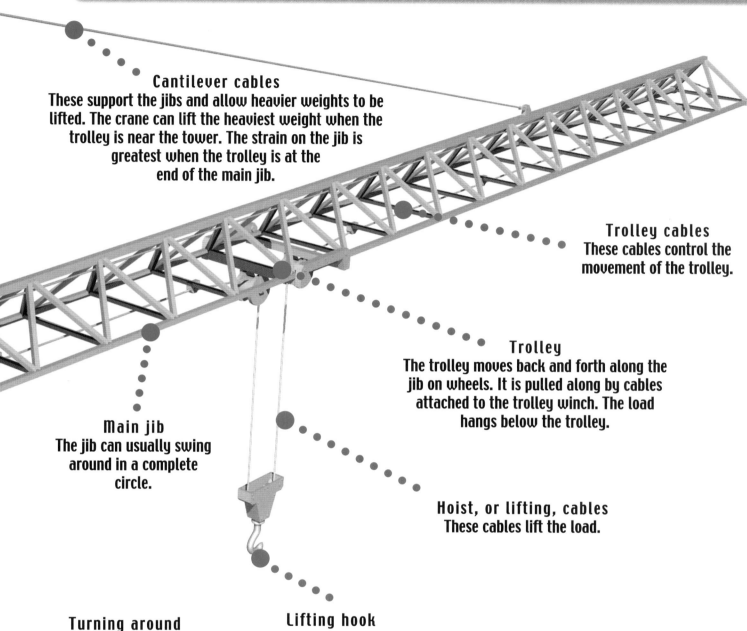

Cantilever cables
These support the jibs and allow heavier weights to be lifted. The crane can lift the heaviest weight when the trolley is near the tower. The strain on the jib is greatest when the trolley is at the end of the main jib.

Trolley cables
These cables control the movement of the trolley.

Trolley
The trolley moves back and forth along the jib on wheels. It is pulled along by cables attached to the trolley winch. The load hangs below the trolley.

Main jib
The jib can usually swing around in a complete circle.

Hoist, or lifting, cables
These cables lift the load.

Lifting hook

Turning around
The crane can swing around in a complete circle on a revolving plate. The plate is turned by an electric motor.

BUILDING SKYSCRAPERS

Tower cranes are the tallest cranes in the world. They are used to help build tall buildings like skyscrapers. They lift things to the top of the building under construction. A tower crane has a long horizontal arm, called a jib, which turns on top of a tall tower. The jib carries a movable trolley, from which the load hangs on steel cables. Electric motors connected to winches wind in the cables attached to the load and trolley. The cables pass around pulleys, which reduce the force needed to lift the load. However, using pulleys increases the length of cable that has to be wound in.

MOBILE CRANE

Telescopic boom
The boom is made in three or four sections. They slide inside each other and are closed up like a telescope when the crane is on the road.

Hydraulic ram
This lifts the boom. It uses pressurized oil to transmit the force of a piston to the boom.

Crane engine
This diesel engine powers the hydraulic system that extends the boom. It also turns the drum to pull in or let out the lifting cables.

Main engine
This diesel engine powers the truck, moving it along at a fairly fast speed. The top speed the crane can reach is 50mph (80kph).

Outrigger
The outriggers are extended outward from the truck and lowered to lift the truck wheels off the ground to support the crane while it is working. Each one has a wide foot that helps spread the weight of the vehicle and its load.

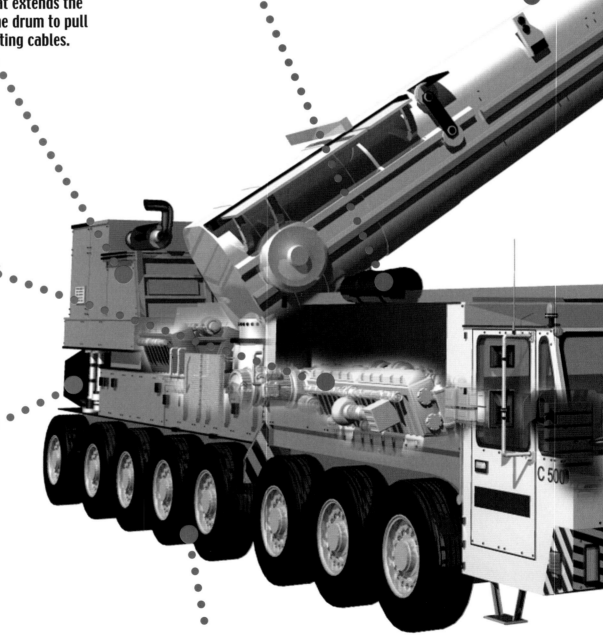

Wheels
The crane is built on the back of a large truck. The truck may have as many as 18 wheels, all of them connected to the steering. When the steering wheel is turned, the back wheels turn at a different angle than the front wheels. This system allows the huge truck to take corners smoothly.

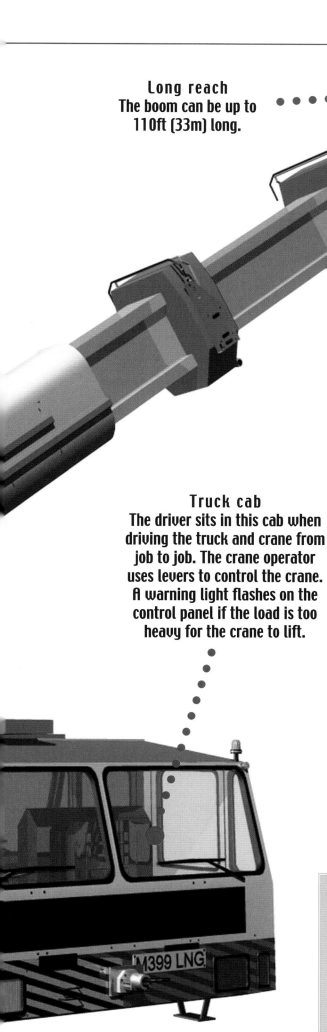

Long reach
The boom can be up to 110ft (33m) long.

Lifting cables
Steel cables lift the load. They are wound in around a drum to raise the load and unwound to lower the load. The cables pass through pulleys, which increase the lifting power of the engine.

Lifting hook
The load is hooked on here for lifting.

Truck cab
The driver sits in this cab when driving the truck and crane from job to job. The crane operator uses levers to control the crane. A warning light flashes on the control panel if the load is too heavy for the crane to lift.

ON THE MOVE

Mobile cranes move from job to job. Renting a mobile crane saves a company from building a crane at the work site, which can take seven days or more and is very expensive. A mobile crane has a long lifting arm, called the jib, or boom, which is drawn in when the crane is on the road. At the work site, the jib is extended. Fully extended, it can reach the top of a six-story building. A mobile crane can weigh 492 tons—as much as 500 family cars—and lift as much as 984 tons.

The world's biggest mobile crane is called *Samson*. It can lift 984 tons on its 625ft (190m) boom. It takes 20 trucks to move *Samson*, and as many as 11 just to haul the counterweights.

KEEPING STEADY

Extending legs called outriggers hold the mobile crane steady while it is lifting. The outriggers extend from each corner of the crane and lift the truck off the ground when it is working. They slide away under the truck when the crane is not being used. To keep the crane from tipping over when the boom is extended, huge weights called counterweights are positioned at the back of the truck. The total amount of counterweight can be as heavy as the crane itself.

DOCKSIDE CRANES

Container crane
A container crane can weigh over 984 tons and stand more than 150ft (48m) high. It can load or unload about 35 containers every hour.

Counterweight
This counterweight balances the weight of the load so that the crane does not fall over.

Trolley cables
These steel cables pull the trolley and load along the boom. The cables are wound and unwound around a drum turned by an electric motor.

Boom
The crane's boom, or arm, can be 200ft (60m) long.

Trolley
The trolley is pulled by steel cables along the boom. The load hangs on cables underneath the trolley.

Support cables
These steel cables support the weight of the load.

Derrick crane
The cargo ship has small cranes, called derrick cranes, on its deck. These can load and unload small pieces of freight.

Working together
Several container cranes may work side by side to unload a large ship. Each ship can carry thousands of containers.

Motor
This moves the crane.

CONTAINER CRANE

At a busy port, huge ships called container ships arrive and depart carrying freight—goods for import or export. The freight is packed in gigantic containers stacked on the deck and in the ship's hold. Cranes that move on railtracks set into the dockside are used to load and unload the containers. The crane's boom swings out over the ship. A trolley moves along the boom until it is above a container. Clamps are lowered on cables from the trolley. The clamps grip the container and the cable is wound in to lift the load. The trolley moves along the boom, carrying the container beneath it. When the container is correctly positioned, it is lowered onto a semi.

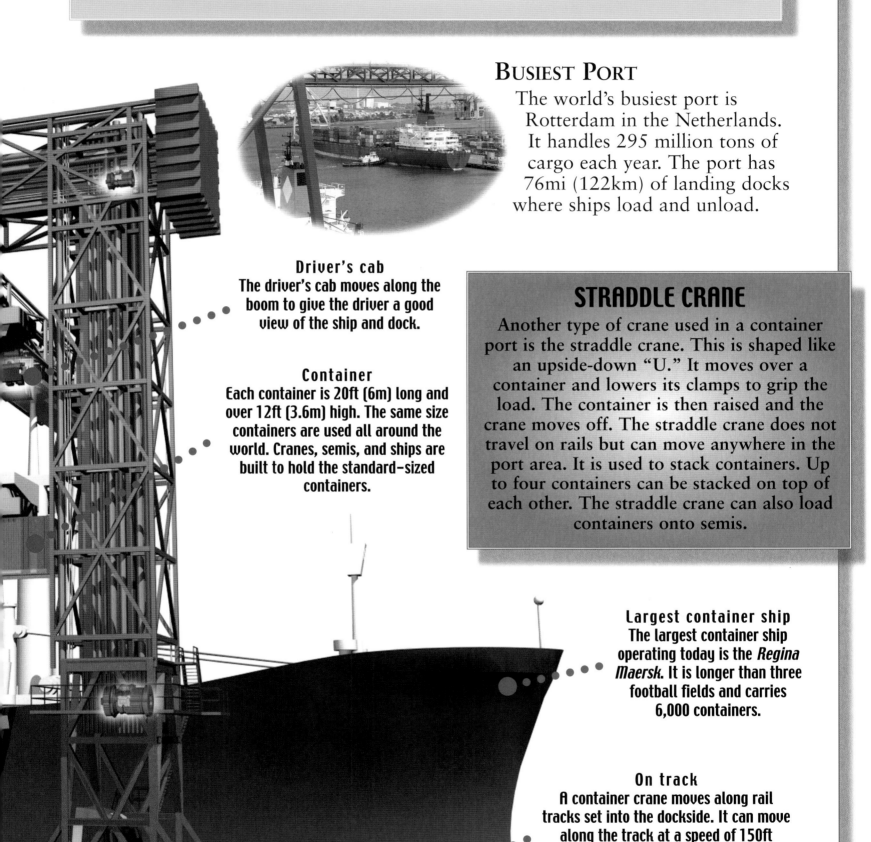

BUSIEST PORT

The world's busiest port is Rotterdam in the Netherlands. It handles 295 million tons of cargo each year. The port has 76mi (122km) of landing docks where ships load and unload.

Driver's cab
The driver's cab moves along the boom to give the driver a good view of the ship and dock.

Container
Each container is 20ft (6m) long and over 12ft (3.6m) high. The same size containers are used all around the world. Cranes, semis, and ships are built to hold the standard-sized containers.

STRADDLE CRANE

Another type of crane used in a container port is the straddle crane. This is shaped like an upside-down "U." It moves over a container and lowers its clamps to grip the load. The container is then raised and the crane moves off. The straddle crane does not travel on rails but can move anywhere in the port area. It is used to stack containers. Up to four containers can be stacked on top of each other. The straddle crane can also load containers onto semis.

Largest container ship
The largest container ship operating today is the *Regina Maersk*. It is longer than three football fields and carries 6,000 containers.

On track
A container crane moves along rail tracks set into the dockside. It can move along the track at a speed of 150ft (46m) per minute.

Truck waiting to be loaded

PAPERMAKING MACHINE

SPECIAL PAPER
Small papermaking machines are used to make special or high-quality paper. This is used in expensive books and presentation scrolls.

Support mesh
Wire mesh supports the wet layer of pulp while the water drains and is sucked out. The web is then strong enough to be lifted off the mesh of wire.

Keeping watch
Workers can walk around the walkway at the top of the machine to keep watch and make repairs.

Felt belt
The felt belt carries the wet web to the press rollers.

Pulp mixture
It takes 12 trees to make about 1 ton of paper.

Suction box
Water is sucked out of the wet pulp here.

Press rollers
These rollers squeeze more water out of the web.

CHINESE PAPER
The Chinese discovered how to make paper about 2,000 years ago. They boiled old fish nets and rags with water, and then beat them to make a soft, wet pulp. A mesh made of fine crisscrossed wires was dipped into the pulp and then removed with a layer of pulp on it. After the water had drained away, the layer of pulp was pressed and dried to make paper.

FROM TREE TO PULP

Today, papermaking is basically the same as it was 2,000 years ago, except that the raw material is wood from trees such as pine and spruce. They are grown in plantations for the paper industry. The papermaking machine was invented in 1803 by two English brothers, Henry and Sealy Fourdrinier. Papermaking machines are sometimes called Fourdrinier machines. First, the bark is stripped from the wood, then the wood is ground to a pulp by giant grinders. The pulp is cooked with chemicals to break it into fibers. Then it is washed, bleached, and beaten to produce smaller, finer fibers. Finally, it is mixed with water and fed into the papermaking machine.

Calender rollers
The calender rollers smooth the surface of the paper.

Heated drying rollers
The heated drying rollers take water out of the paper in the form of steam.

Long machine
Papermaking machines are over 650ft (200m) long and can produce more than 295 tons of paper in a day. Over 3,280ft (1,000m) of paper races through the machine every minute.

Jumbo
The paper is wound on a large reel called a jumbo. It can be attached and removed without stopping the machine.

Computer control panels
A computer checks the strength, thickness, and color of the paper. Only a few people are needed to look after the huge machine.

MAKING PAPER

In a papermaking machine, the wet pulp is spread on a wire mesh that turns on rollers. The mesh vibrates and the water drains out of the pulp, leaving a smooth layer of fibers, called the web. The web passes onto a moving belt made of felt. Then it goes through a series of rollers called press rollers, which squeeze out more water. The web then passes between heated drying cylinders, which remove the remaining water. Finally, the web passes through an upright stack of rollers, called the calender, which smooth its surface.

PRINTING PRESS

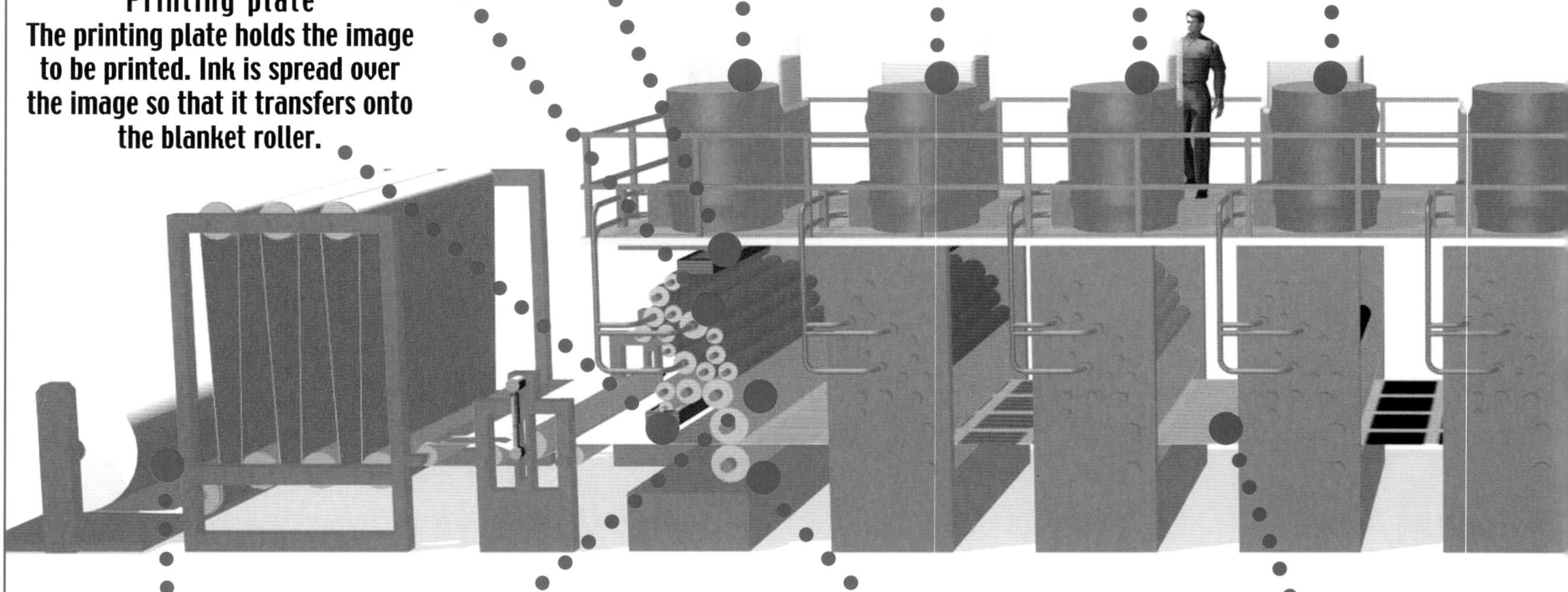

Inking rollers
There are different kinds of inking roller. Some have a rubber surface, others have a metal surface. They make sure that ink is spread evenly over the plate.

Ink trough
Each of the four presses has a trough that holds the ink.

Printing press 1 prints cyan (blue).

Printing press 2 prints magenta (red).

Printing press 3 prints yellow.

Printing press 4 prints black.

Printing plate
The printing plate holds the image to be printed. Ink is spread over the image so that it transfers onto the blanket roller.

Reel of paper
In an automated press, the reel can be changed without stopping the press.

Blanket roller
The rubber-coated blanket roller transfers the image from the plate to the paper. Its rubber surface prints evenly on the bumpy surface of the paper.

Transfer roller
The transfer roller carries the paper to the next printing plate. Mechanical grippers on the transfer drum hold the paper accurately in place so that the four colors are printed in register (in the correct place).

Paper web
The web, a continuous strip of paper, is fed through the press.

LETTERPRESS

Johann Gutenberg, a German goldsmith, invented printing using movable type in 1439. Individual letters were carved into small wooden blocks—the type. The blocks were placed in a frame, wiped with ink, and pressed onto paper to produce the printed page. This process is called letterpress printing. It is still used today, although offset lithography, shown here, is now much more common.

PRINTING SHEETS

Small printing presses print sheets of paper. Sheet-fed machines are used for printing books that require good-quality printing, unlike the machines used by many magazines and newspapers which are not intended to be kept for long.

LITHOGRAPHY

In lithography, a thin metal sheet called a plate, or stereo, is used to print pages. An image of the text and pictures to be printed is formed photographically on the plate. The plate is treated with chemicals to make ink stick to the dark parts of the image. The plate is often wrapped around a cylinder which rotates at high speed. As the cylinder rotates, the plate is pressed against paper coming off a large reel. The ink transfers to the paper, forming the printed image. In a similar process called offset lithography, the image is first transferred to a rubber cylinder, called the blanket roller, which then prints onto paper.

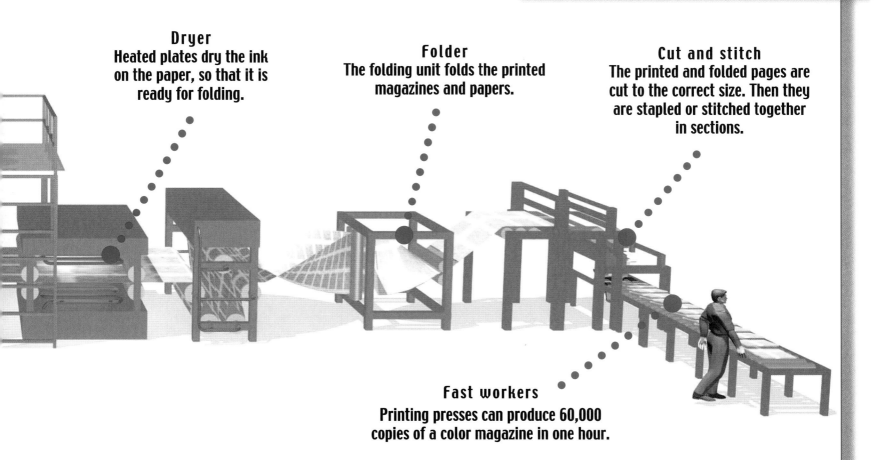

Dryer
Heated plates dry the ink on the paper, so that it is ready for folding.

Folder
The folding unit folds the printed magazines and papers.

Cut and stitch
The printed and folded pages are cut to the correct size. Then they are stapled or stitched together in sections.

Fast workers
Printing presses can produce 60,000 copies of a color magazine in one hour.

PRINTING A PICTURE

Printed pictures are produced using a pattern of small dots of ink. There are many dots where the picture is dark and fewer where the picture is light. This allows the light and dark shades of the picture to be reproduced. To print a full-color picture, four separate plates are made. One plate prints the cyan (blue) parts of the picture. Other plates print the magenta (red), yellow, and black parts. All the colors in a picture can be reproduced using only these four colors.

ROADMAKING MACHINES

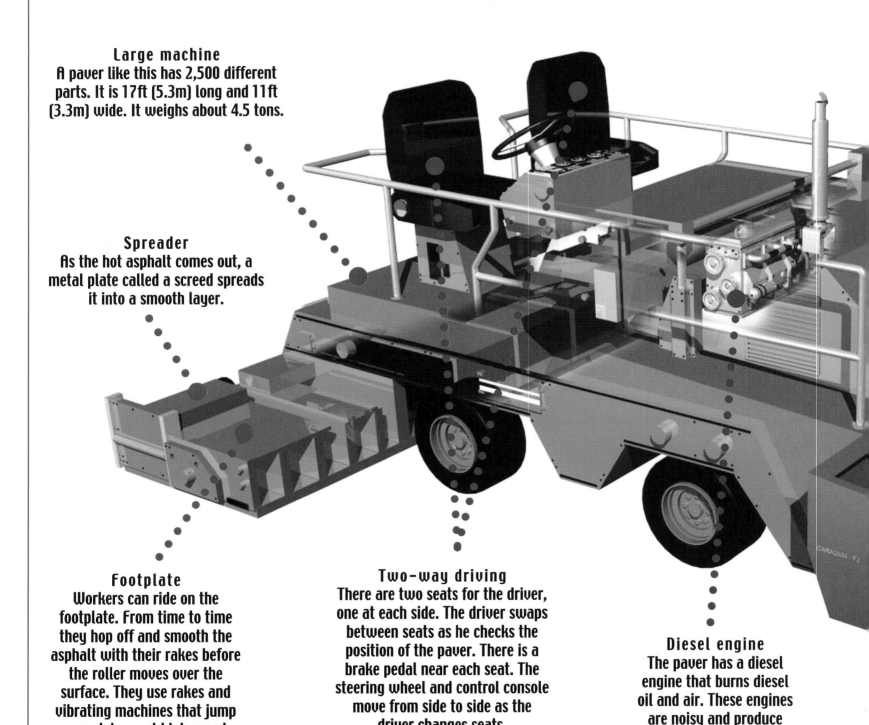

Large machine
A paver like this has 2,500 different parts. It is 17ft (5.3m) long and 11ft (3.3m) wide. It weighs about 4.5 tons.

Spreader
As the hot asphalt comes out, a metal plate called a screed spreads it into a smooth layer.

Footplate
Workers can ride on the footplate. From time to time they hop off and smooth the asphalt with their rakes before the roller moves over the surface. They use rakes and vibrating machines that jump up and down at high speed, banging the ground flat.

Two-way driving
There are two seats for the driver, one at each side. The driver swaps between seats as he checks the position of the paver. There is a brake pedal near each seat. The steering wheel and control console move from side to side as the driver changes seats.

Diesel engine
The paver has a diesel engine that burns diesel oil and air. These engines are noisy and produce lots of fumes.

SMELLY MACHINE

The roadmaking machine is a hot and stinking giant. It is also known as a road or track paver. Its job is to spread a layer of hot asphalt on the surface of a new or repaired road. Asphalt is a mixture of tar and crushed rock. The asphalt has to be kept hot until it is spread on the road, otherwise it would set hard and clog up the paver. The hot asphalt has a horrible smell.

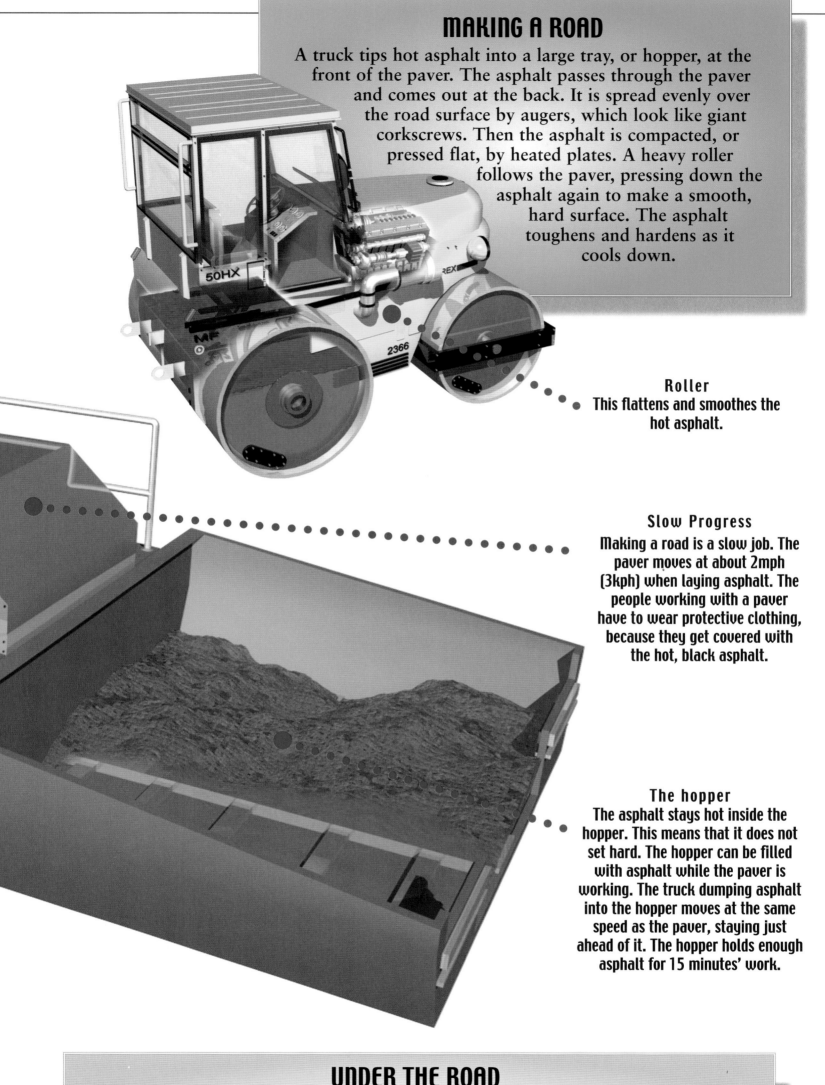

MAKING A ROAD

A truck tips hot asphalt into a large tray, or hopper, at the front of the paver. The asphalt passes through the paver and comes out at the back. It is spread evenly over the road surface by augers, which look like giant corkscrews. Then the asphalt is compacted, or pressed flat, by heated plates. A heavy roller follows the paver, pressing down the asphalt again to make a smooth, hard surface. The asphalt toughens and hardens as it cools down.

Roller
This flattens and smoothes the hot asphalt.

Slow Progress
Making a road is a slow job. The paver moves at about 2mph (3kph) when laying asphalt. The people working with a paver have to wear protective clothing, because they get covered with the hot, black asphalt.

The hopper
The asphalt stays hot inside the hopper. This means that it does not set hard. The hopper can be filled with asphalt while the paver is working. The truck dumping asphalt into the hopper moves at the same speed as the paver, staying just ahead of it. The hopper holds enough asphalt for 15 minutes' work.

UNDER THE ROAD

The asphalt is laid on a foundation of layers of crushed stone called aggregate. There is a thick layer of large stones at the bottom. The stones are compacted by heavy rollers. Then a thinner layer of smaller stones is placed on top and compacted.

GLASSMAKING MACHINE

Measured amounts
The sand, soda, and other ingredients have to be weighed carefully and mixed in batches. If they are mixed in the wrong proportions, the glass will be low quality.

Frit hopper
A mixture of sand, soda, and lime (called frit) and waste glass (called cullet) is fed into the furnace. Soda is sodium carbonate. It lowers the melting point of sand. Lime is calcium carbonate. It keeps the glass from dissolving in water. Sand is mainly silica or silicon dioxide—it is the material glass is made from.

Furnace
Jets of flame stream from the sides of the furnace. The temperature in the furnace rises to 2,894°F (1,590°C), and melts the ingredients.

Continuous sheet of glass
The molten glass emerges from the furnace and runs onto the molten tin, forming a thin layer or sheet.

Bath of molten tin
The molten tin is kept in an oxygen-free atmosphere. Otherwise the tin would react with oxygen, and oxidize. This would make the surface of the glass uneven.

HOW GLASSMAKING WAS DISCOVERED

Glass was first made by the Egyptians around 5,000 years ago. They probably discovered how to make it by accident. Someone might have lit a fire on a sandy beach and later found shiny beads of glass in the ashes. The heat of the fire would have turned sand into glass. For this to happen, the fire must have been built on sand mixed with soda, a substance left behind when sea water evaporates in the sun. Soda helps the sand to melt and turn into glass. Today glass is made by melting soda and other sodium compounds with sand in a glassmaking machine.

FLOAT GLASS PROCESS

Glass for windows and doors is produced as flat sheets. Sheet glass was once made by flattening lumps of molten glass between rollers. But this process produced sheets with an uneven surface. Today, most sheet glass is made by the float glass process. Molten glass is floated on top of a huge bath of molten tin. The surface of the glass is very smooth because the surface of the molten tin is perfectly smooth. There are 170 float glass plants in the world. Each day they produce 3,000mi (4,800km) of glass. In a year, they make a ribbon of glass over 1,000,000mi (1,600,000km) long.

BOTTLEMAKING

Bottles are made using a mold. A lump of molten glass is put into a bottle-shaped mold and compressed air is then forced in. This pushes the glass into the shape of the mold. The bottle is then removed and left to cool.

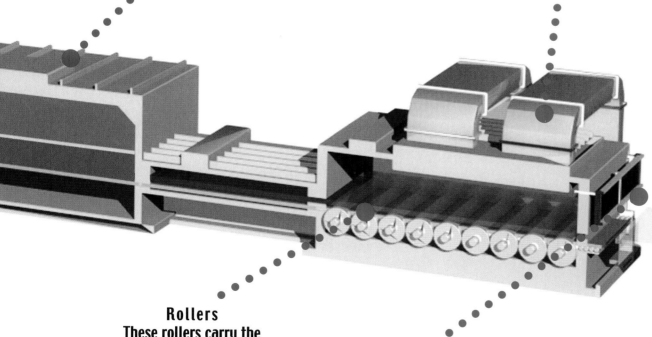

Temperature-controlled cooling section
The glass is cooled slowly, to prevent it from cracking or breaking when it is cut into sheets.

Water jets
The sheets are washed by water jets.

Big sheets
The glass sheets can be up to 20ft (6m) long and 10ft (3m) wide.

Rollers
These rollers carry the glass to the cutter.

Cutter
The glass is cut into lengths with a diamond-tipped cutter.

Strong stuff
Although a glass sheet is easy to break, a fine glass fiber is five times stronger than steel. Automatic stackers offload the glass sheets, then overhead cranes take the sheets to the warehouse for storage.

THE LONDON EYE

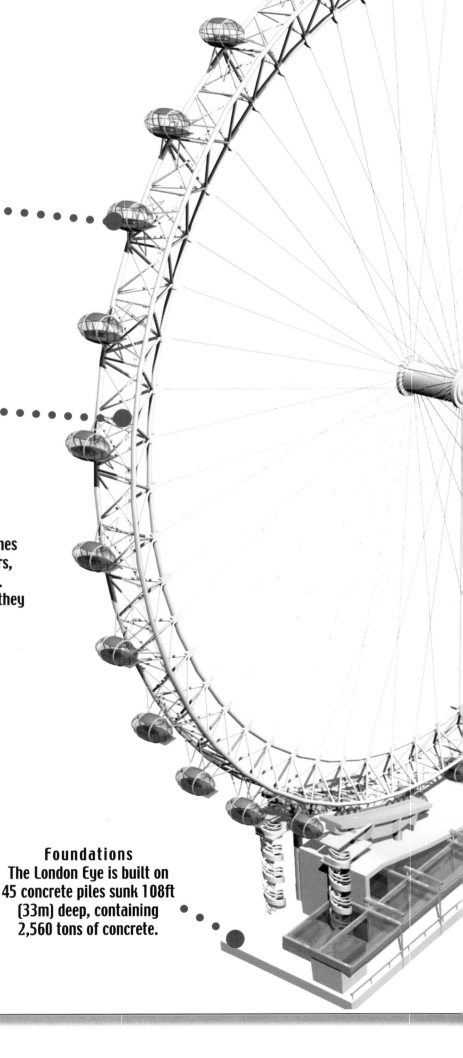

Inside an egg
The 32 fully-enclosed, egg-shaped passenger cars, or capsules, each weigh about 9 tons and hold 25 people. The capsules are attached to the outer rim, and each one has an individual motor to rotate it as the wheel goes around. They are heated in the winter and air-conditioned in the summer.

Round and round
One circuit of the wheel takes half an hour.

By the river
The London Eye is located on the south bank of the Thames River in London, England. Although built to last 50 years, the wheel only has planning permission for five years. After that, Londoners will have to decide whether or not they want to keep it.

MONSTER TOURIST ATTRACTION

The London Eye was built as a tourist attraction to bring people to London for the Millennium celebrations. The 1,475-ton structure is heavier than 250 double-decker buses.

At night, the London Eye pulses gently with soft light—at 16 pulses a minute—our natural rate of breathing.

Foundations
The London Eye is built on 45 concrete piles sunk 108ft (33m) deep, containing 2,560 tons of concrete.

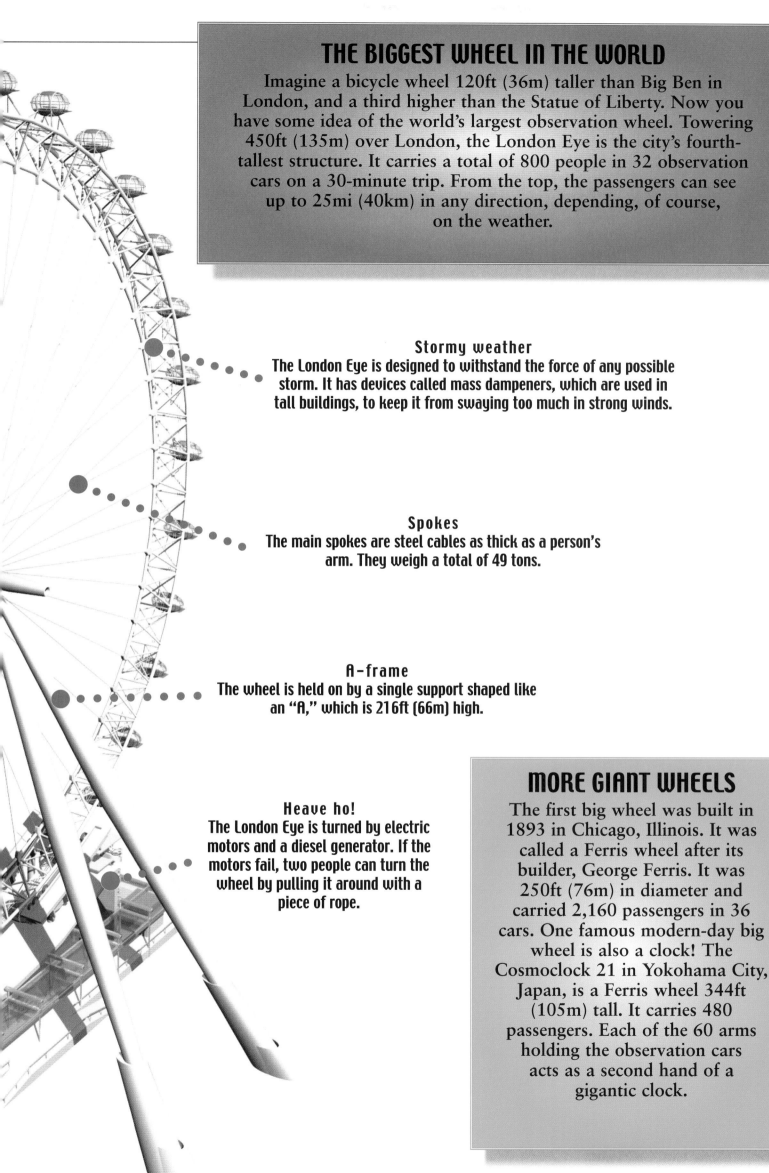

THE BIGGEST WHEEL IN THE WORLD

Imagine a bicycle wheel 120ft (36m) taller than Big Ben in London, and a third higher than the Statue of Liberty. Now you have some idea of the world's largest observation wheel. Towering 450ft (135m) over London, the London Eye is the city's fourth-tallest structure. It carries a total of 800 people in 32 observation cars on a 30-minute trip. From the top, the passengers can see up to 25mi (40km) in any direction, depending, of course, on the weather.

Stormy weather
The London Eye is designed to withstand the force of any possible storm. It has devices called mass dampeners, which are used in tall buildings, to keep it from swaying too much in strong winds.

Spokes
The main spokes are steel cables as thick as a person's arm. They weigh a total of 49 tons.

A-frame
The wheel is held on by a single support shaped like an "A," which is 216ft (66m) high.

Heave ho!
The London Eye is turned by electric motors and a diesel generator. If the motors fail, two people can turn the wheel by pulling it around with a piece of rope.

MORE GIANT WHEELS
The first big wheel was built in 1893 in Chicago, Illinois. It was called a Ferris wheel after its builder, George Ferris. It was 250ft (76m) in diameter and carried 2,160 passengers in 36 cars. One famous modern-day big wheel is also a clock! The Cosmoclock 21 in Yokohama City, Japan, is a Ferris wheel 344ft (105m) tall. It carries 480 passengers. Each of the 60 arms holding the observation cars acts as a second hand of a gigantic clock.

FLIGHT SIMULATOR

Computer
The computer makes sure that the simulator moves like a real aircraft in response to the trainee pilot's actions. It also records a training session, so that the instructor and trainee pilot can learn from it afterward.

Instructor's console
The instructor sits at a console behind the trainee pilot. The console displays information about the pilot's performance. The instructor can tell the computer to simulate special conditions, such as foggy weather, or to give the trainee a difficult task, such as an emergency landing.

Pistons
The pistons tilt and roll the simulator to follow the pilot's commands. If the pilot pulls up on the joystick, the simulator tilts up to show that the airplane would tilt up. The pistons can also create the effect of air turbulence by making the simulator vibrate up and down.

LEARNING TO FLY

Trainee pilots can learn to fly an airplane without leaving the ground. They are trained on a computer-controlled flight simulator. This is a copy of a real cabin in which the trainee pilot sits. The simulator has all the control buttons and instruments found in a real airplane cockpit, and the pilot "flies" the simulator exactly as if it were the real thing. The computer makes the simulator react like an airplane—it tilts and rolls as the pilot moves the controls, and the instruments give realistic readings of such things as height and the amount of fuel left in the tanks. The simulator even reproduces the engine noise and the sound of air flowing past the airplane.

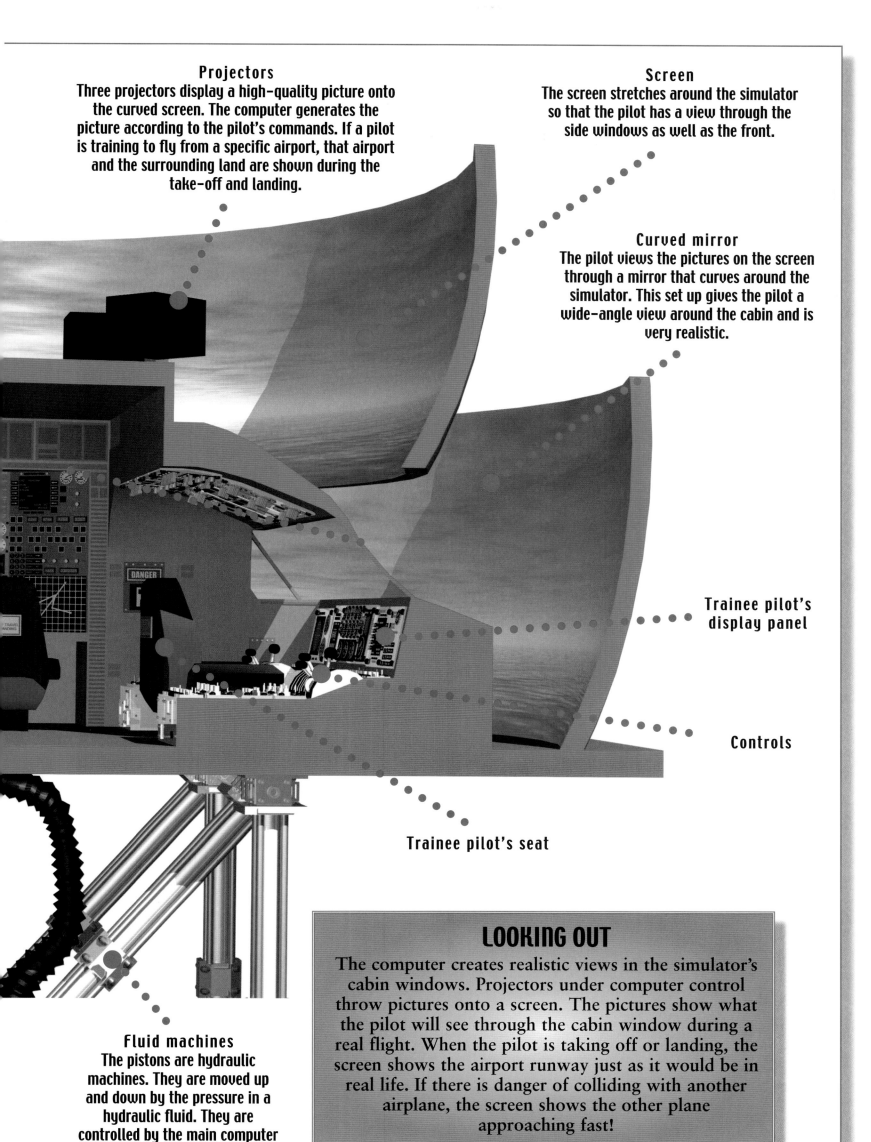

Projectors
Three projectors display a high-quality picture onto the curved screen. The computer generates the picture according to the pilot's commands. If a pilot is training to fly from a specific airport, that airport and the surrounding land are shown during the take-off and landing.

Screen
The screen stretches around the simulator so that the pilot has a view through the side windows as well as the front.

Curved mirror
The pilot views the pictures on the screen through a mirror that curves around the simulator. This set up gives the pilot a wide-angle view around the cabin and is very realistic.

Trainee pilot's display panel

Controls

Trainee pilot's seat

Fluid machines
The pistons are hydraulic machines. They are moved up and down by the pressure in a hydraulic fluid. They are controlled by the main computer and respond to the trainee pilot's actions.

LOOKING OUT

The computer creates realistic views in the simulator's cabin windows. Projectors under computer control throw pictures onto a screen. The pictures show what the pilot will see through the cabin window during a real flight. When the pilot is taking off or landing, the screen shows the airport runway just as it would be in real life. If there is danger of colliding with another airplane, the screen shows the other plane approaching fast!

ROLLER COASTER

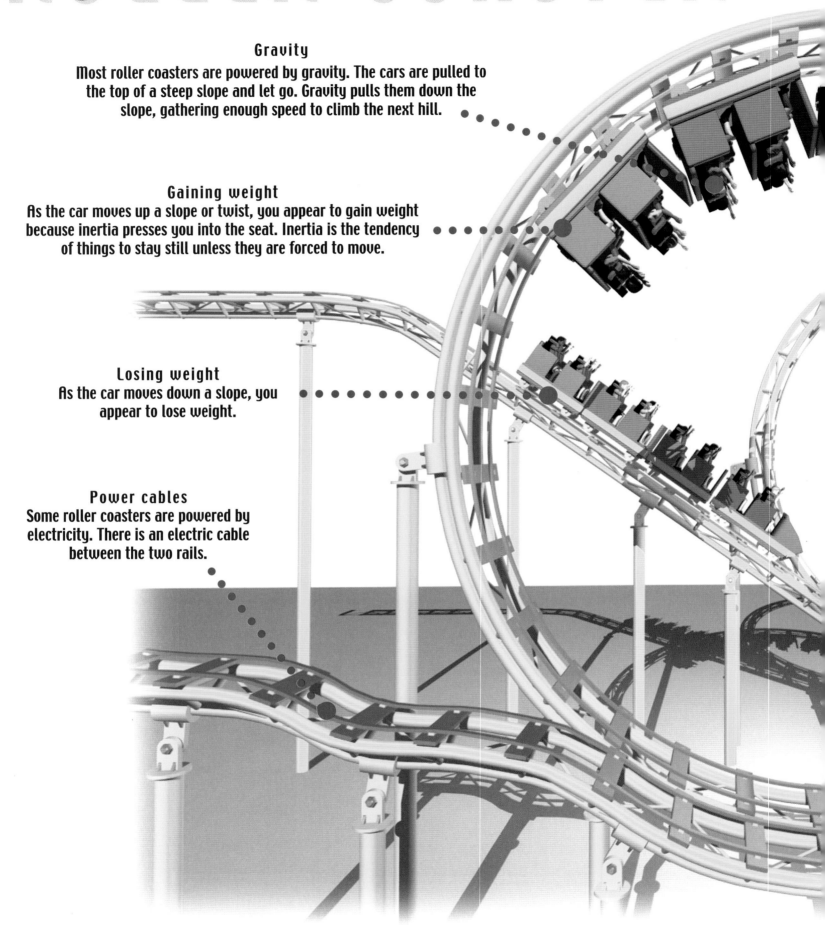

Gravity
Most roller coasters are powered by gravity. The cars are pulled to the top of a steep slope and let go. Gravity pulls them down the slope, gathering enough speed to climb the next hill.

Gaining weight
As the car moves up a slope or twist, you appear to gain weight because inertia presses you into the seat. Inertia is the tendency of things to stay still unless they are forced to move.

Losing weight
As the car moves down a slope, you appear to lose weight.

Power cables
Some roller coasters are powered by electricity. There is an electric cable between the two rails.

MOMENTUM
When a roller coaster suddenly dives down, your stomach seems to get "left behind." This is because anything moving tends to keep going in one direction. This tendency is called momentum. If you were not strapped into your seat, momentum would continue to carry you uphill, and you would be thrown into the air as the car hurtled down.

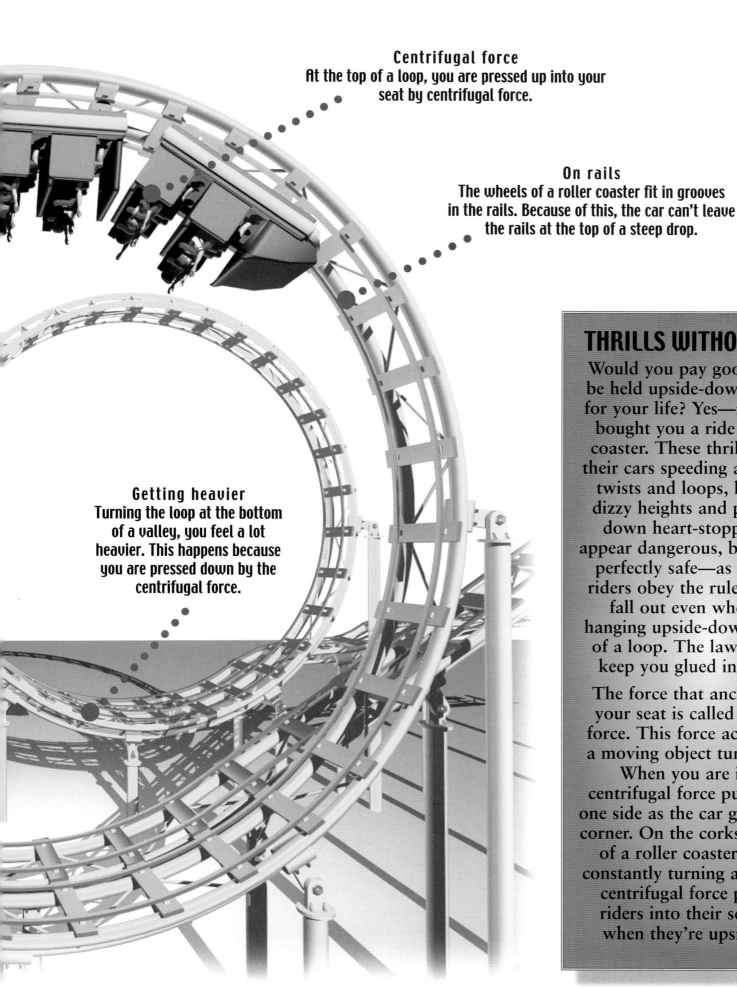

Centrifugal force
At the top of a loop, you are pressed up into your seat by centrifugal force.

On rails
The wheels of a roller coaster fit in grooves in the rails. Because of this, the car can't leave the rails at the top of a steep drop.

Getting heavier
Turning the loop at the bottom of a valley, you feel a lot heavier. This happens because you are pressed down by the centrifugal force.

THRILLS WITHOUT SPILLS

Would you pay good money to be held upside-down screaming for your life? Yes—if the money bought you a ride on a roller coaster. These thrill rides with their cars speeding around crazy twists and loops, hurtling up dizzy heights and plummeting down heart-stopping drops appear dangerous, but are in fact perfectly safe—as long as the riders obey the rules. You can't fall out even when you're hanging upside-down at the top of a loop. The laws of science keep you glued in your seat.

The force that anchors you in your seat is called centrifugal force. This force acts whenever a moving object turns a corner. When you are in a car, centrifugal force pushes you to one side as the car goes around a corner. On the corkscrew section of a roller coaster, the car is constantly turning a corner. The centrifugal force presses the riders into their seats—even when they're upside-down!

HIGHEST, FASTEST, LONGEST

The highest and fastest roller coaster in the world is called *Superman—The Escape*. It is at Six Flags Magic Mountain in Valencia, California. The cars reach a speed of 100mph (161kph). The structure is 1,650 feet (503m) tall. The longest roller coaster in the world is at Lightwater Valley Theme Park in Ripon, England. Called *The Ultimate*, the ride is almost 2mi (3km) long.

CHURCH ORGAN

WIND INSTRUMENT

Church organs are wind instruments. Sound is produced by blowing air into pipes of different lengths and diameters. The length of the pipe determines the pitch of the note. The long pipes also have a large diameter, and therefore produce the loudest sounds. The organist plays a keyboard, with each key sounding a different note. An organ can also play chords, made up of several notes that harmonize, or blend, smoothly together. Chords can be produced by operating the stops—the knobs at the side of the keyboards.

Pedal pipes

Stops
When a stop is pulled out, a slider blocks off the openings of some pipes. Pressing a key on the keyboard will then let air flow only to the unblocked pipes. This means that different combinations of notes can be sounded when the same key is pressed.

Keyboard or manual
There are usually three keyboards, called the swell, the great, and the choir. Each keyboard is linked to a set of pipes with the same name. When a key is pressed, air flows through the pipe linked to that key.

Choir pipes
These pipes are connected to the choir keyboard. They produce the highest-pitched notes.

Organist's seat

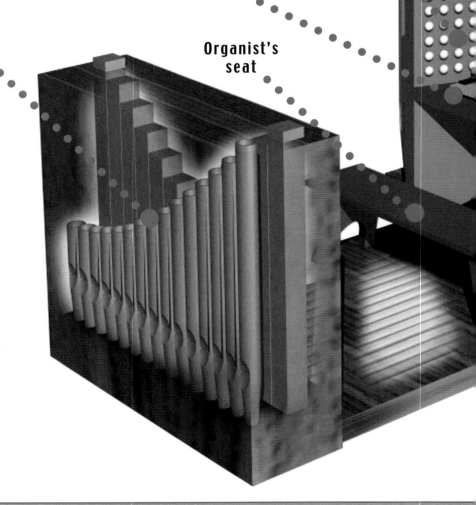

PIPES, KEYBOARDS, AND PEDALS

The organ has three main parts—the wind supply, the keyboards, and the pipes. The wind, or air, supply is blown through the pipes by fans or bellows operated by an electric motor. Most organs have two or three keyboards, but some have four or five, and one famous organ has six! Each keyboard is linked to a different set of pipes. There are three sets of pipes—swell, great, and choir.

Great pipes
These pipes are connected to the great keyboard.

Pipes
There are two kinds of pipes in each set—the flue tone pipes and the reed tone pipes. They each produce a different musical effect, even when the same note is played.

Windchest
The windchest holds the pressurized air from the blower before it flows through the pipes.

Swell pipes
These pipes are connected to the swell keyboard.

BIG AND LOUD

The church or cathedral organ is the biggest musical instrument around. Some church organs are over 50ft (15m) tall and have thousands of pipes. Some of these pipes are smaller than a pencil, and others are large enough for a person to fit inside.

Pedals
The pedals form a keyboard for the feet to play. They are connected to a set of pipes called the pedal pipes. There are also pedals that produce special musical effects.

FLOOD BARRIER

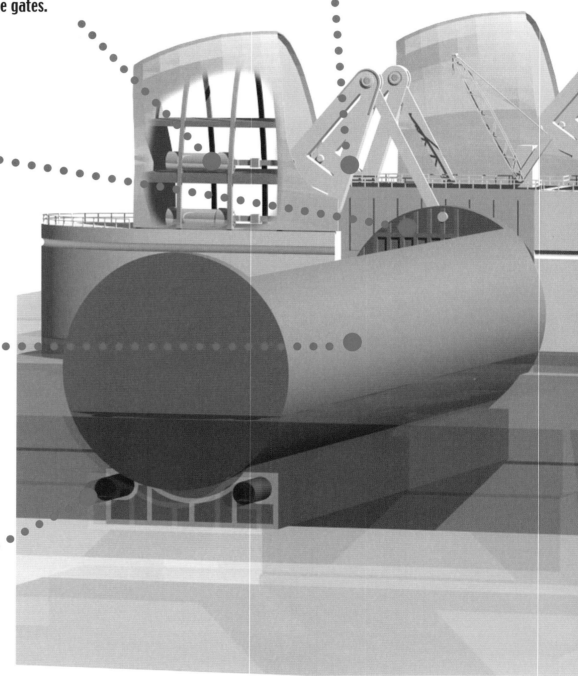

Lifting mechanism
This is the rocker beam and arm which raises the gate. The beam is moved by two hydraulic cylinders.

Hydraulic ram
A piston in a large cylinder applies pressure to a liquid. The liquid transmits the force to the rocker beam and lifting arm. This system, called a hydraulic ram, magnifies the force applied to the piston to lift the gates.

Locking the gate
A latch mechanism locks the gate in position.

Gate
The four largest gates are 216ft (66m) wide and weigh 1,480 tons each. They are covered with steel plating 1.5in (40mm) thick. Wooden strips protect the gates in case ships collide with them.

Power and control cables
Tunnels carry power and control cables between the piers and the control room on the riverbank.

HOLDING BACK THE TIDE

For centuries, the city of London, England has been in danger of sudden floods. At very high tides, the Thames River can break through its banks and flood the low-lying parts of the city. Now, a mighty machine, the Thames Flood Barrier, has been designed to prevent flooding. The Thames Barrier is like a huge wall built across the river to hold back the tide. The Barrier is 1,715ft (523m) wide. It has four main gates, each as high as a five-story building, which are normally left open to let shipping through.

OPENING AND CLOSING THE GATES

The gates in the Thames Barrier lie on the bed of the river when they are open. This means that ships can move over the gates and through the barrier. If a very high tide is expected, the gates are raised to block the river. The gates are rotated or turned in a semi-circle to lift them from the riverbed. A large mechanical arm, or beam, at the end of each gate lifts it. The beams are powered hydraulically, like the arms of a mechanical excavator. At the time of they were made, the hydraulic cylinders used in the barrier were the largest in the world.

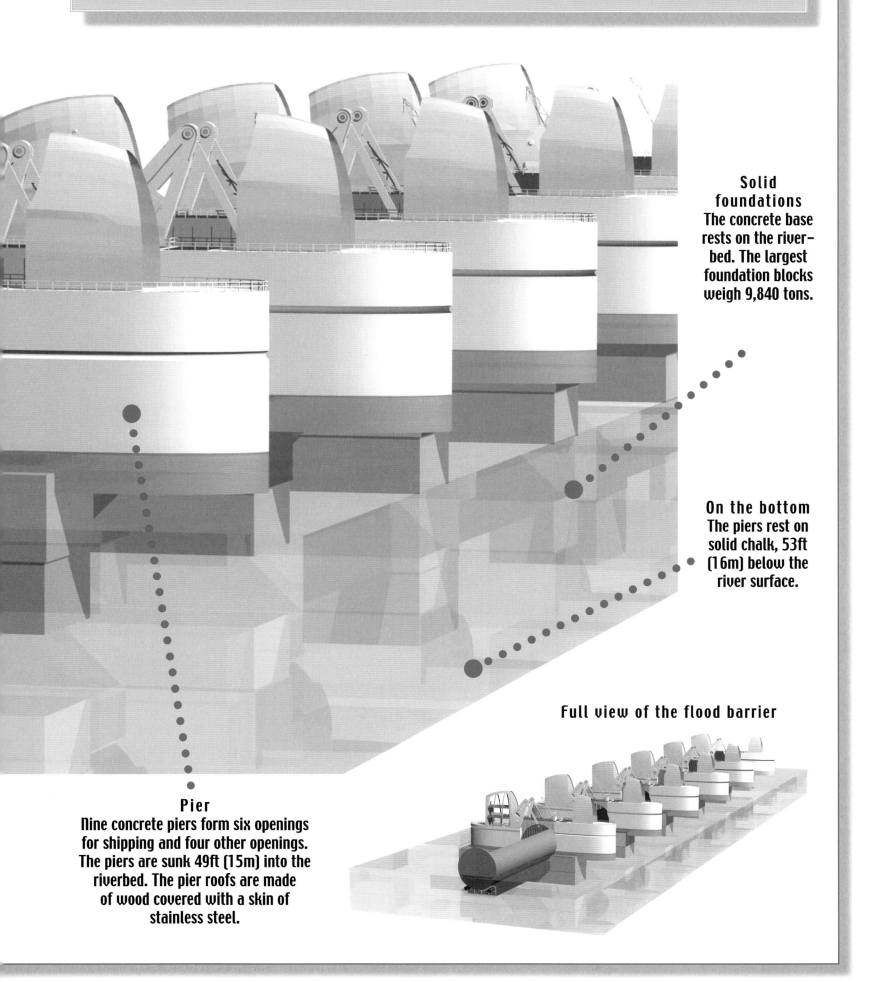

Solid foundations
The concrete base rests on the river-bed. The largest foundation blocks weigh 9,840 tons.

On the bottom
The piers rest on solid chalk, 53ft (16m) below the river surface.

Full view of the flood barrier

Pier
Nine concrete piers form six openings for shipping and four other openings. The piers are sunk 49ft (15m) into the riverbed. The pier roofs are made of wood covered with a skin of stainless steel.

OIL RIG

PLUMBING THE DEPTHS

The world consumes over 68 million barrels of oil a day. Much of it comes from large oil rigs, or platforms, scattered across the oceans of the world. These rigs either float on the sea or stand on the seabed. They drill into the seabed to the oil deposits beneath it. The oil is pumped to the surface and carried by tanker or pipeline to refineries on land. Natural gas is often found with the oil and can be extracted at the same time.

Gas purification system
The natural gas that comes to the surface with the crude oil is a mixture of gases. The useful part of the mixture is taken out, turned into a liquid, and sent ashore.

BRANCHING OUT

A system called directional drilling allows wells to be drilled at different angles instead of straight down. This means that many oil fields can be reached from one rig. A single rig can receive oil from up to 60 wells.

Rig support legs
The legs house the drill that digs its way down to the oil field. Once a well has been drilled, the legs contain the pipes carrying oil, gas, and water. The oil and gas are separated and purified. The gas is pumped to the mainland through pipes. When the pipeline is shut down, the gas is burned, or flared, off.

KINDS OF RIGS

A floating rig, or semi-submersible platform, rests on huge floats called pontoons. It is held in place above the oil well by steel cables that anchor each corner of the platform to the seabed. Some rigs, called guyed tower platforms, stand on a steel framework that reaches down to the seabed. The tower is anchored to the seabed with steel cables. Gravity platforms are the biggest and heaviest. These huge concrete structures rest directly on the seabed, held in place by their sheer weight. A platform is like a small town. It has its own power supply, water supply, living quarters, helicopter pad, and medical facilities. Oil workers may live and work on the rigs for weeks at a time.

The tallest oil rig is the *Mars* platform in the Gulf of Mexico. It rises 2,940ft (896m) from the seabed to the surface. It stands twice as high as the Empire State Building. The *Mars* platform produces 38,000 barrels of oil per day.

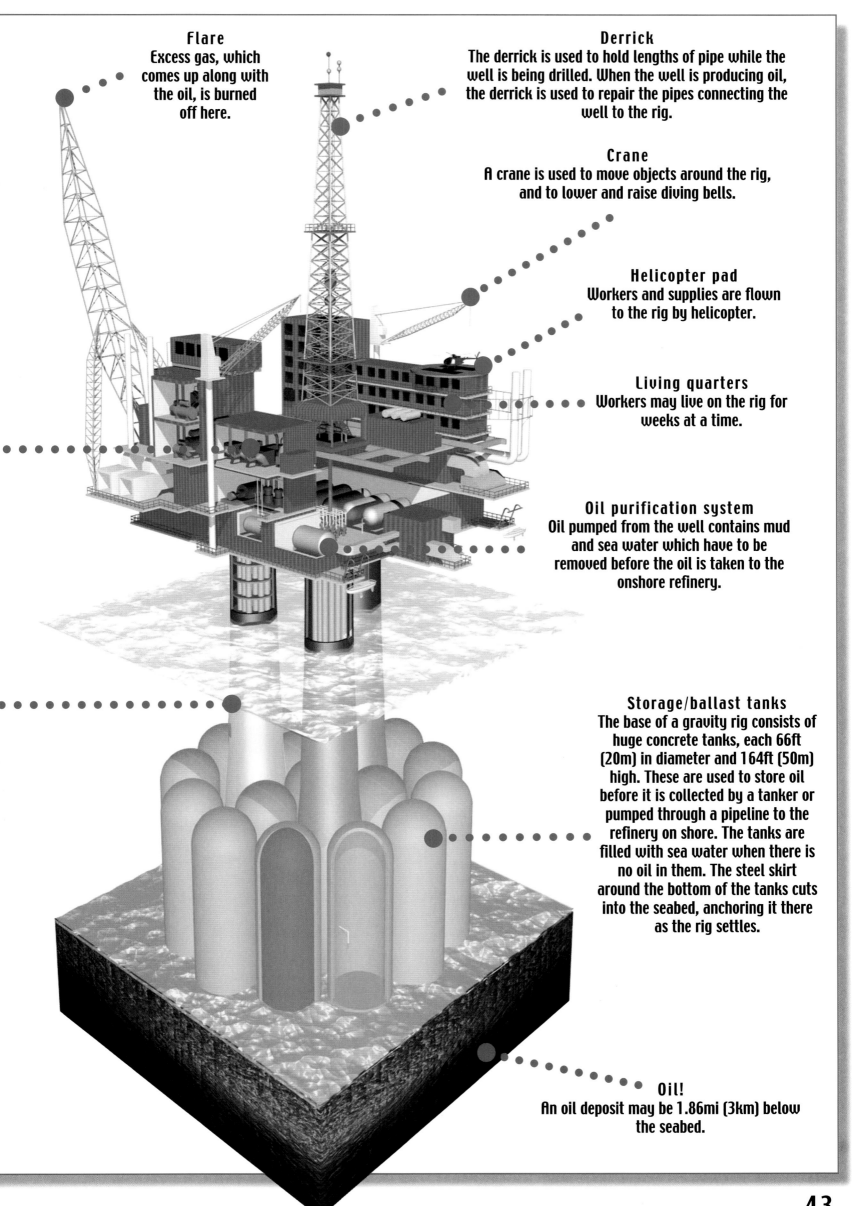

Flare
Excess gas, which comes up along with the oil, is burned off here.

Derrick
The derrick is used to hold lengths of pipe while the well is being drilled. When the well is producing oil, the derrick is used to repair the pipes connecting the well to the rig.

Crane
A crane is used to move objects around the rig, and to lower and raise diving bells.

Helicopter pad
Workers and supplies are flown to the rig by helicopter.

Living quarters
Workers may live on the rig for weeks at a time.

Oil purification system
Oil pumped from the well contains mud and sea water which have to be removed before the oil is taken to the onshore refinery.

Storage/ballast tanks
The base of a gravity rig consists of huge concrete tanks, each 66ft (20m) in diameter and 164ft (50m) high. These are used to store oil before it is collected by a tanker or pumped through a pipeline to the refinery on shore. The tanks are filled with sea water when there is no oil in them. The steel skirt around the bottom of the tanks cuts into the seabed, anchoring it there as the rig settles.

Oil!
An oil deposit may be 1.86mi (3km) below the seabed.

TURBOGENERATOR

Power take-off cables
The electricity produced flows along the take-off cables and into the transmission system to homes, factories, and offices. Large turbogenerators can produce electricity with a strength of up to 30,000 volts.

More than one
Power stations usually have more than one turbogenerator. The steam is fed through each machine, one after the other, until all its energy has been extracted.

Generating giants
A turbogenerator can be up to 80ft (24m) long and 20ft (6m) high.

Rotor
The rotating coil, or rotor, is made up of many coils of wire that turn between the stator (magnet) coils. Electricity is produced in the rotor coils by magnetism from the stator. In large generators, the rotor turns 3,600 times each minute.

TURBINE AND GENERATOR

A turbogenerator is a huge machine—20 feet by 20 feet by 79 feet. It is made of two connected parts—a turbine and a generator. The turbine is like a windmill. It has many blades that turn as the high-pressure steam flows over them. The turbine turns the generator. The generator produces electricity as it turns.

The world's largest turbogenerator is at the Ignalina power station in Lithuania. It produces 1,450 million watts of power—enough for over 400,000 homes.

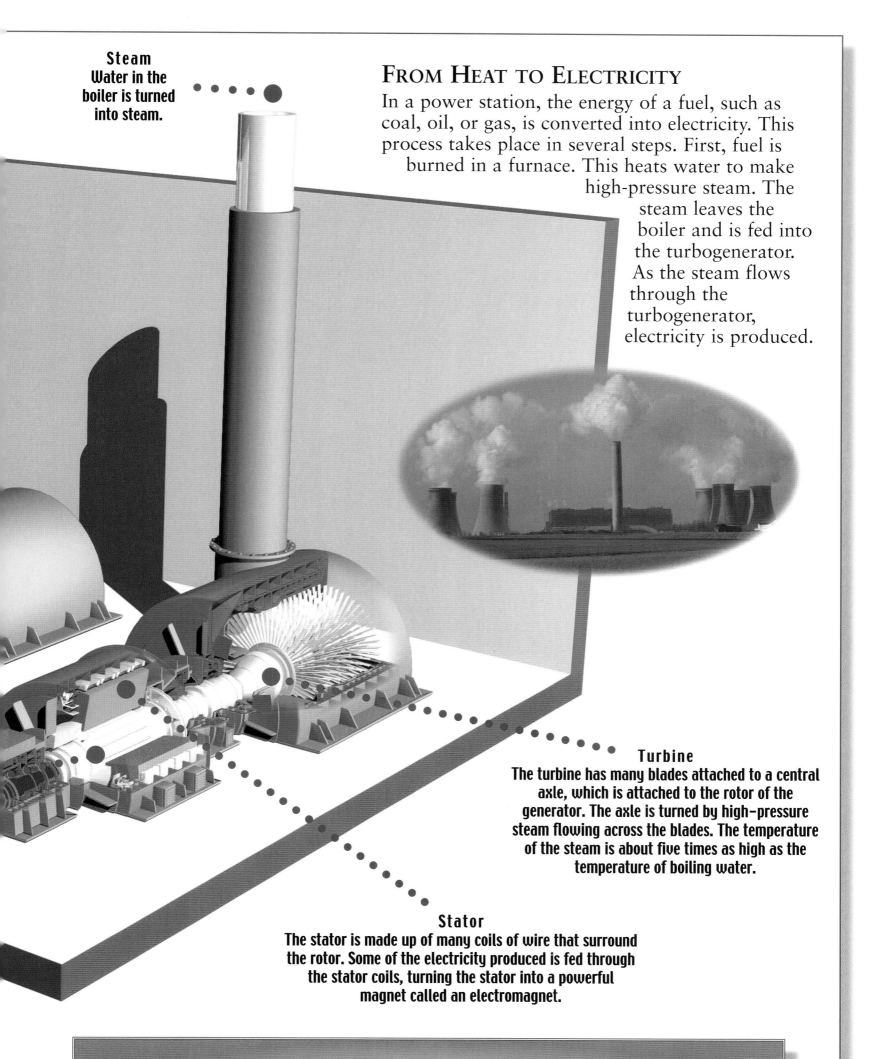

Steam
Water in the boiler is turned into steam.

FROM HEAT TO ELECTRICITY

In a power station, the energy of a fuel, such as coal, oil, or gas, is converted into electricity. This process takes place in several steps. First, fuel is burned in a furnace. This heats water to make high-pressure steam. The steam leaves the boiler and is fed into the turbogenerator. As the steam flows through the turbogenerator, electricity is produced.

Turbine
The turbine has many blades attached to a central axle, which is attached to the rotor of the generator. The axle is turned by high-pressure steam flowing across the blades. The temperature of the steam is about five times as high as the temperature of boiling water.

Stator
The stator is made up of many coils of wire that surround the rotor. Some of the electricity produced is fed through the stator coils, turning the stator into a powerful magnet called an electromagnet.

MAGNETISM AND ELECTRICITY

A generator uses magnetism to produce electricity. When a wire moves near a magnet, electricity flows in the wire. Inside the generator, a coil of wire is spun near a strong magnet. An electric current is produced in the coil. The coil is also called the rotor because it spins, or rotates. The magnet does not move. It is called the stator because it is stationary, or still.

HYDROELECTRIC POWER STATION

SUDDEN DEMAND

Power stations have to boost power supplies when the demand for electricity suddenly increases. The hydroelectric power station is able to do this by allowing more water to flow through the turbine.

Dam

Most dams are curved to withstand the enormous pressure of the water in the reservoir. The dam wall is thickest at the bottom. The world's highest dam is the Nurek dam on the Vakhsh River in Tajikistan. It is 984ft (300m) from top to bottom.

Sluice gate

The sluice gate is opened to let water flow from the reservoir to the turbines. The water flow can be increased or reduced by adjusting the position of the sluice gate. Most power is produced when the sluice gate is wide open.

POWER FROM WATER

Water power was used thousands of years ago, and it still plays an important part in modern life. Watermills have ground grain for over 2,000 years. Around 200 years ago, water power was used in the first factories to run machines such as looms for weaving cloth. Today, water power produces electricity in hydroelectric power stations. Huge dams hold back the water of a river, which builds up into a reservoir or lake behind the dam. Water from the reservoir is allowed to flow through a giant turbine—the modern equivalent of a watermill. An electricity generator is connected to the turbine. Electricity is produced when the generator is turned by the turbine.

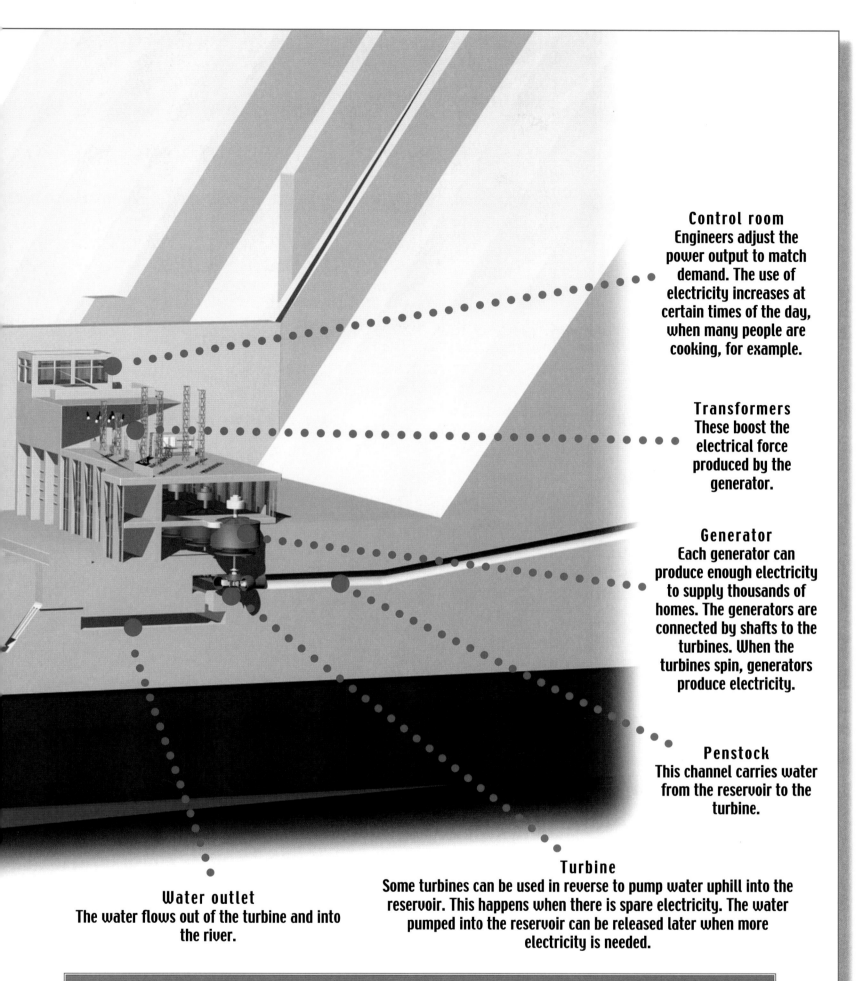

Control room
Engineers adjust the power output to match demand. The use of electricity increases at certain times of the day, when many people are cooking, for example.

Transformers
These boost the electrical force produced by the generator.

Generator
Each generator can produce enough electricity to supply thousands of homes. The generators are connected by shafts to the turbines. When the turbines spin, generators produce electricity.

Penstock
This channel carries water from the reservoir to the turbine.

Turbine
Some turbines can be used in reverse to pump water uphill into the reservoir. This happens when there is spare electricity. The water pumped into the reservoir can be released later when more electricity is needed.

Water outlet
The water flows out of the turbine and into the river.

THE TURBINE

A modern turbine is designed to be as energy-efficient as possible. Inside the turbine, the water pushes against the turbine blades, making them spin at high speed as it spirals horizontally toward the center. When the maximum amount of energy has been harnessed, the water flows away through an outlet in the center of the turbine and into the river.

The world's most powerful hydroelectric station is at Itaipu on the Paraná River near the border between Brazil and Paraguay. It produces 13,320 million watts of power, which is 10 times as much as an average oil- or gas-fired power station.

NUCLEAR POWER STATION

Boiler
The hot water from the reactor is carried to the boiler, where it turns the water inside the boiler into high-pressure steam.

Reactor pressure vessel
The reactor pressure vessel contains the reactor. Water flows through the reactor at high pressure, absorbing heat. It then enters the boiler, turning the water inside the boiler into steam.

Generator
The generator is turned by the rotating turbine and produces electricity. The electricity is sent to homes, factories, and offices along metal cables called transmission lines.

Generator room
This room houses the turbines and generators. There are usually at least three turbines and generators.

Turbine
High-pressure steam from the boiler spins the turbine blades as it flows through the turbine. The turbine is connected to the generator.

Pump house

Control room
The power station is controlled by computers as well as by people. The computers control the reactor by lowering and raising the control rods.

MAKING ELECTRICITY

A nuclear power station works like a coal- or gas-fired power station. In these stations, coal or gas is burned to heat water and produce high-pressure steam. The steam turns a propeller or turbine. The turbine powers a generator, which produces electricity. But in a nuclear power station, the fuel used to heat the water is uranium. Uranium is not burned like coal or oil. Instead, its atoms are split in a process called nuclear fission. This process produces the heat energy to turn the water into steam and power the turbines.

SPLITTING ATOMS

All materials are made up of very small particles called atoms. At the center of each atom is a dense ball of matter called the nucleus. The nucleus of a uranium atom can be split when it is hit by a small particle called a neutron. When this happens, energy is released and more neutrons are produced. These neutrons go on to split other uranium nuclei in a chain reaction, causing a continuous release of intense heat.

Fuel rods
The fuel rods contain the uranium fuel.

Control rod
The rods are lowered or raised to control the nuclear reaction. They absorb neutrons and slow down the nuclear reaction when they are lowered.

Solid foundations
The reactor is built on strong foundations to prevent damage by earthquakes.

Containment vessel
Made of thick concrete, this surrounds the reactor pressure vessel. It is designed to keep dangerous radiation from escaping in an emergency.

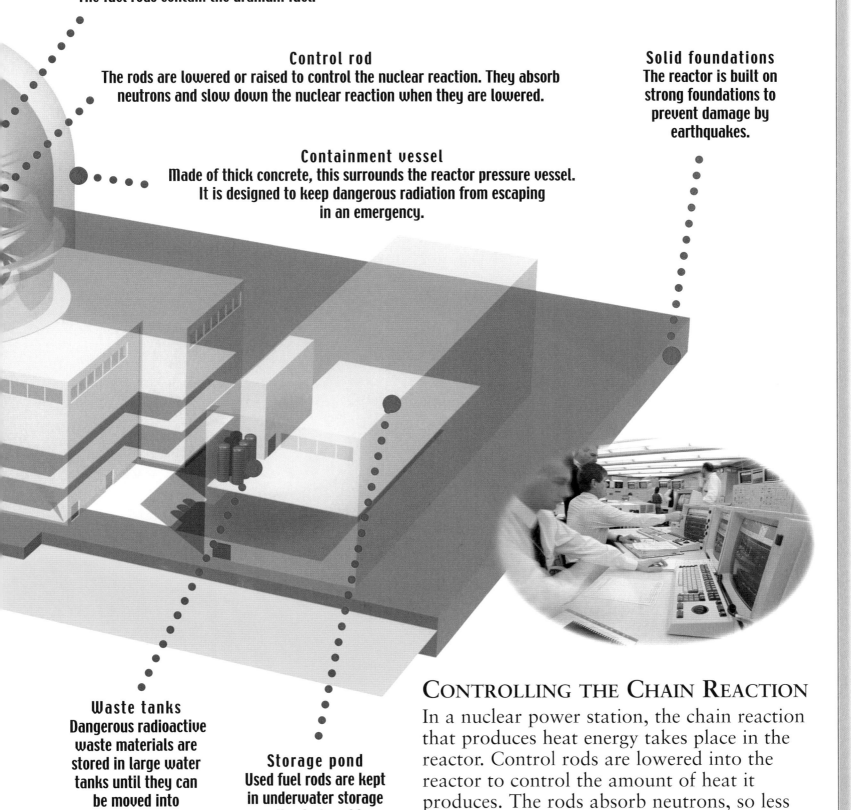

Waste tanks
Dangerous radioactive waste materials are stored in large water tanks until they can be moved into underground storage areas.

Storage pond
Used fuel rods are kept in underwater storage units, designed to prevent dangerous radiation leaks.

CONTROLLING THE CHAIN REACTION

In a nuclear power station, the chain reaction that produces heat energy takes place in the reactor. Control rods are lowered into the reactor to control the amount of heat it produces. The rods absorb neutrons, so less energy is produced when they are lowered, and more when they are raised.

WIND TURBINE

WIND FARMS

A wind farm is a collection of wind turbines built on a high ridge, sea coast, or open plain. There may be hundreds of wind turbines in a wind farm. The largest wind farms generate as much electricity as three power stations. There are around 20,000 wind turbines producing electricity in the world today.

Gearbox
A gearbox links the turbine blades to the electricity generator. The gearbox ensures that the generator turns at a high speed whatever the wind speed. When the wind is weak and turns the turbine blades slowly, the gearbox increases the speed of the generator.

Control system
The control system automatically adjusts the direction and angle of the blades. This is important because the maximum amount of power must be extracted from the wind.

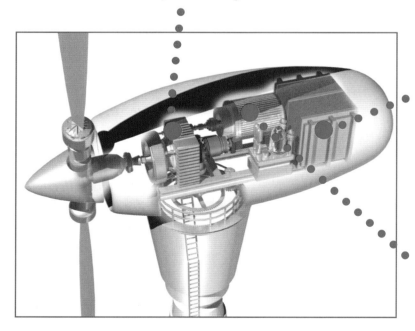

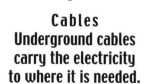

Generator
The generator produces electricity. Inside the generator a coil of wire turns near a magnet. An electric current is produced in the coil.

Cables
Underground cables carry the electricity to where it is needed.

POWER FROM THE WIND
For over 5,000 years, the wind has been used as a source of power. Windmills grind corn. Modern versions of the windmill generate electricity. These wind turbines, as they are called, have huge blades to catch the slightest wind. The blades are connected to an electricity generator. When the blades are turned by the wind, this turns the generator and produces electricity.

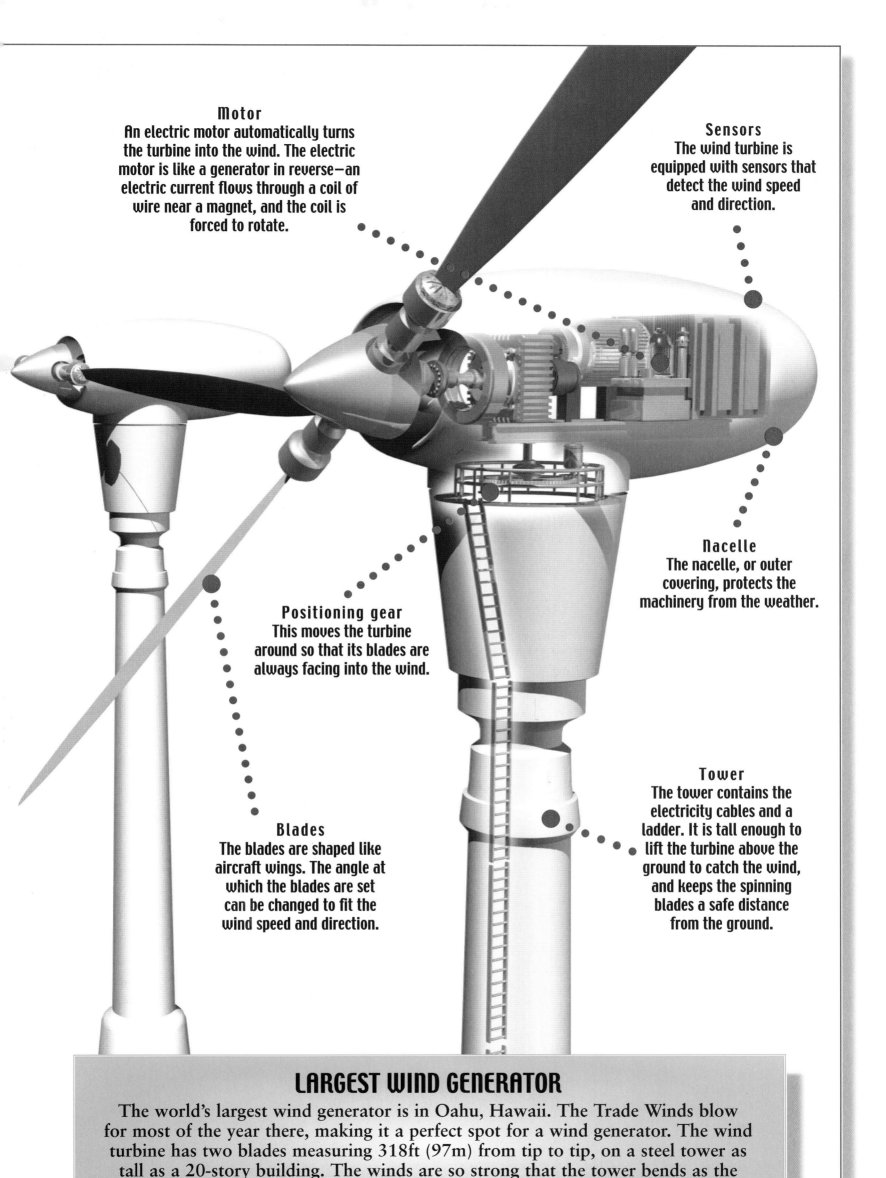

Motor
An electric motor automatically turns the turbine into the wind. The electric motor is like a generator in reverse—an electric current flows through a coil of wire near a magnet, and the coil is forced to rotate.

Sensors
The wind turbine is equipped with sensors that detect the wind speed and direction.

Positioning gear
This moves the turbine around so that its blades are always facing into the wind.

Nacelle
The nacelle, or outer covering, protects the machinery from the weather.

Blades
The blades are shaped like aircraft wings. The angle at which the blades are set can be changed to fit the wind speed and direction.

Tower
The tower contains the electricity cables and a ladder. It is tall enough to lift the turbine above the ground to catch the wind, and keeps the spinning blades a safe distance from the ground.

LARGEST WIND GENERATOR

The world's largest wind generator is in Oahu, Hawaii. The Trade Winds blow for most of the year there, making it a perfect spot for a wind generator. The wind turbine has two blades measuring 318ft (97m) from tip to tip, on a steel tower as tall as a 20-story building. The winds are so strong that the tower bends as the winds blow. The wind turbine generates enough power for 1,000 homes.

INDUSTRIAL ROBOT

Electricity cables

Sensor
Robot arms contain sensors that detect where the arm is and feed this information into the computer control unit. The computer checks that the arm is in the correct position. If not, the computer activates the motors to move the arm.

Computer unit
The computer holds the program that guides the robot arm. It receives information from the arm sensors and controls the motors that move the arm.

Robot hand
Car assembly robots can be equipped with many different kinds of tools—welding units, nozzles for spraying paint, sanding discs for smoothing surfaces, and electromagnets for lifting metal parts.

CARMAKING ROBOTS
Most of the world's robots are used to make cars. Each robot performs a single task on the car chassis as it moves along the production line.

HARD WORKERS
The popular idea of a robot is a machine that looks and acts like a human. But most robots are industrial robots, and don't look like us at all. The industrial robot is a computer-controlled mechanical arm. Robot arms can bend in every direction. At the end of the arm is the robot "hand." This is a tool such as a welder, paint sprayer, or gripper for grasping objects. These robots work around the clock in factories, doing jobs like welding metal parts together and painting the finished products. They live up to their name, since the word "robot" comes from the Czech word for a slave.

ROBOT EYES

Some robots are fitted with vision units, or "eyes," to increase their usefulness. A welding robot without vision must have the parts it is welding placed in exactly the right position. But a robot with vision can check the position of the parts and adjust its actions accordingly.

Welding metal
Welding is a process that joins pieces of metal together. The edges of the metal pieces are melted so that they flow together. Welding robots use a strong electric current to melt the metals.

Robot arm
The arm has shoulder, elbow, and wrist joints that can move in any direction.

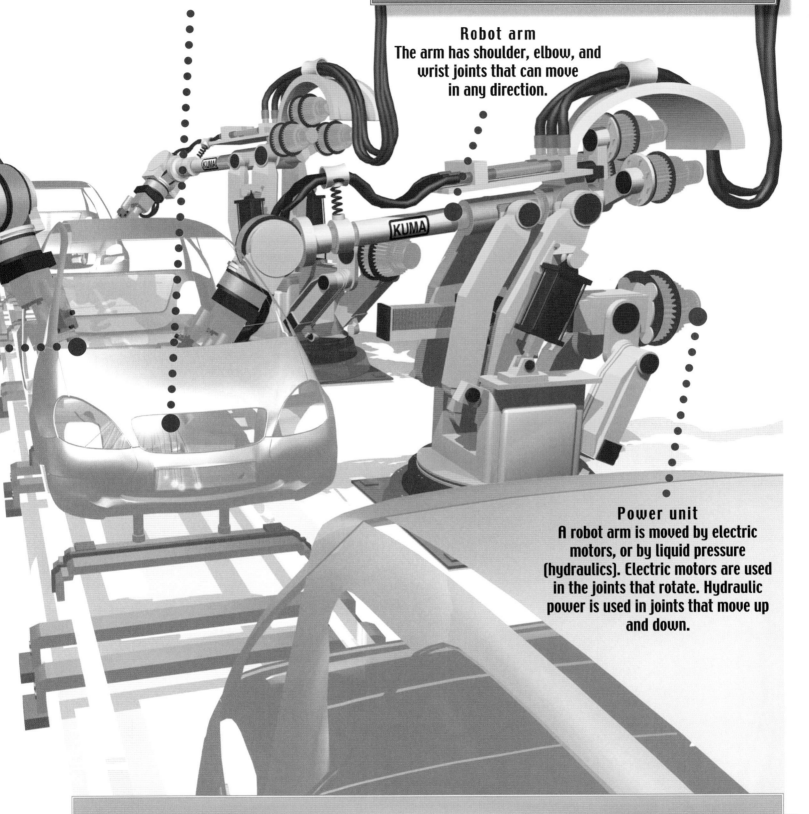

Power unit
A robot arm is moved by electric motors, or by liquid pressure (hydraulics). Electric motors are used in the joints that rotate. Hydraulic power is used in joints that move up and down.

TEACHING A ROBOT

An industrial robot has to be programmed like a computer, to tell it what to do. There are two main ways of instructing industrial robots. The first is to work out exactly what movements are needed to complete a task, and to write these movements into a program for the control computer. The second is to teach the robot a job such as painting, by guiding its arm through the movements needed to complete the task. The robot is programmed to remember what it has been taught, and will repeat the movements exactly.

RADIO TELESCOPE

RADIO WAVES FROM SPACE

Astronomers can figure out how stars, galaxies, and black holes behave by studying the radio waves that they produce. The radio waves coming from outer space are collected by radio telescopes. The main kind of radio telescope looks like a giant dish. The dish focuses the radio waves onto a sensitive radio receiver. The radio signal is amplified (made stronger) by the telescope's electronic circuits, and displayed on a computer screen.

Radio receiver
The radio receiver can be tuned to different signals, just as a home radio can be tuned to different radio stations. Hot, bright stars and hydrogen gas in space produce strong signals. The receiver contains amplifying circuits that increase the size of the signal received.

GIANT TELESCOPES

The world's largest radio telescope is in Arecibo in Peurto Rico. Its dish is built into a small circular valley and is 1,000ft (305m) across, wider than three football fields. It can pick up signals 1 trillion times weaker than a small light bulb. The world's largest fully steerable radio telescope is in the Effelsberger Valley, in Germany. It is a dish 328ft (100m) across and weighs almost 3,000 tons.

Large collecting dish
Radio telescopes need to be larger than ordinary telescopes (which collect light) because radio waves are much longer than light waves. The bigger the dish, the more detail it can detect.

WORKING TOGETHER

Several telescopes can be connected together to produce a much clearer picture of the sky. The largest of these combined instruments, known as interferometers, is the Australia Telescope. It has three dishes—one in Australia, another in Japan, and a third in orbit around the Earth. This interferometer is equivalent to a radio telescope with a diameter of 17,100mi (27,523km)—over twice the diameter of the Earth.

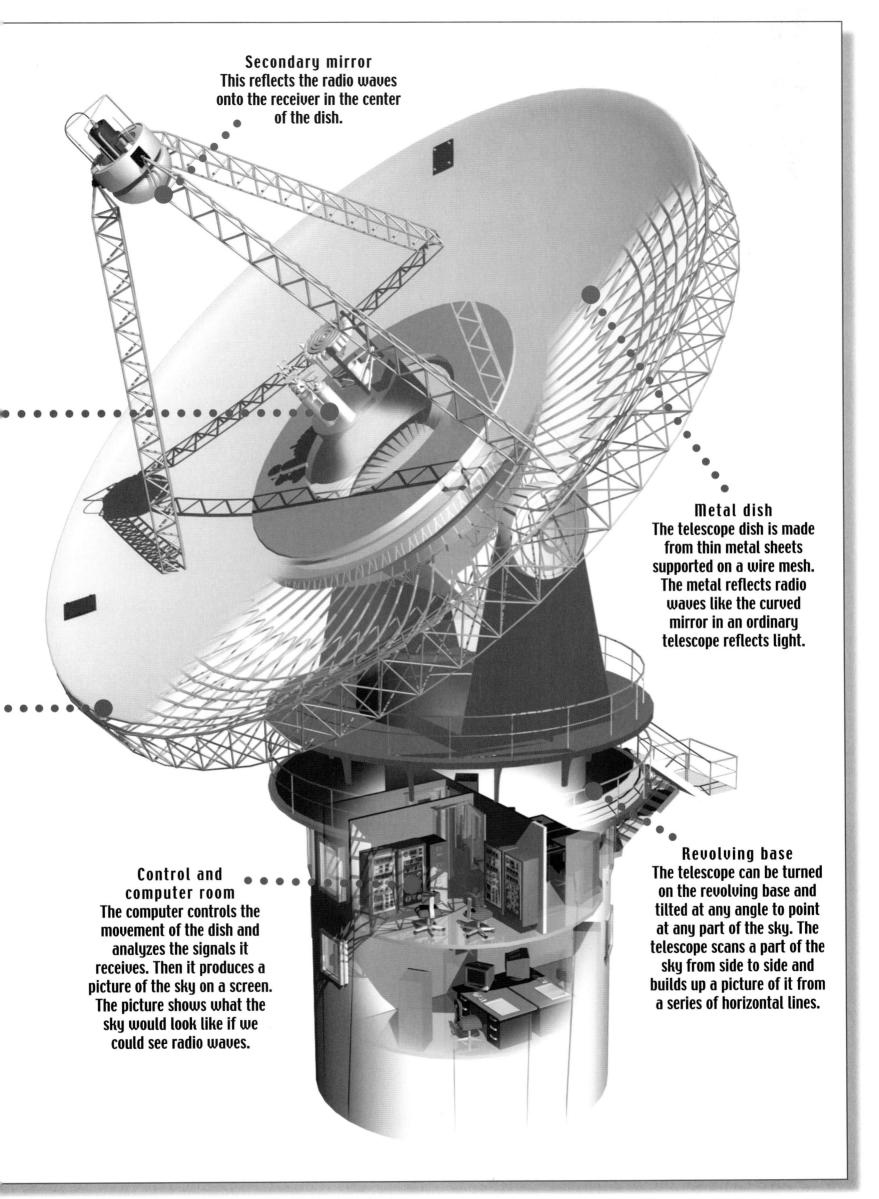

Secondary mirror
This reflects the radio waves onto the receiver in the center of the dish.

Metal dish
The telescope dish is made from thin metal sheets supported on a wire mesh. The metal reflects radio waves like the curved mirror in an ordinary telescope reflects light.

Control and computer room
The computer controls the movement of the dish and analyzes the signals it receives. Then it produces a picture of the sky on a screen. The picture shows what the sky would look like if we could see radio waves.

Revolving base
The telescope can be turned on the revolving base and tilted at any angle to point at any part of the sky. The telescope scans a part of the sky from side to side and builds up a picture of it from a series of horizontal lines.

NASA CRAWLER-TRANSPORTER

Operator's cabin
Two operator's cabins, one at each end of the chassis, are used to steer the crawler. The cabins have the world's largest windshield wipers—each is 3.5ft (106cm) long.

Water cooling radiator
Water is cooled in the radiator, which is like a giant car-cooling radiator. The water is then circulated around the engine to keep it cool.

Generator
There are four electricity generators. Two of these produce the power for the electric motors that drive the crawler. The other two are used for jacking, steering, and ventilating the two cabins and engine control room.

LARGEST TRACKED VEHICLE

This crawler-transporter is the biggest tracked vehicle in the world. It belongs to NASA, and is used to move the Space Shuttle from its hangar to the launch site. This vehicle is a real monster—131ft (40m) wide and 115ft (35m) long. Its top deck, or platform, is the size of a baseball field. The crawler cost $12.3 million to build.

Tracks
The crawler runs on four double tracks like bulldozer tracks at each corner. That's 32 tracks in total. Each track is 68ft (21m) long and 10ft (3m) high. A track weighs over 49 tons, and has 57 "shoes," each weighing 1 ton. Because of the important job they do, the shoes are nicknamed "The Golden Slippers."

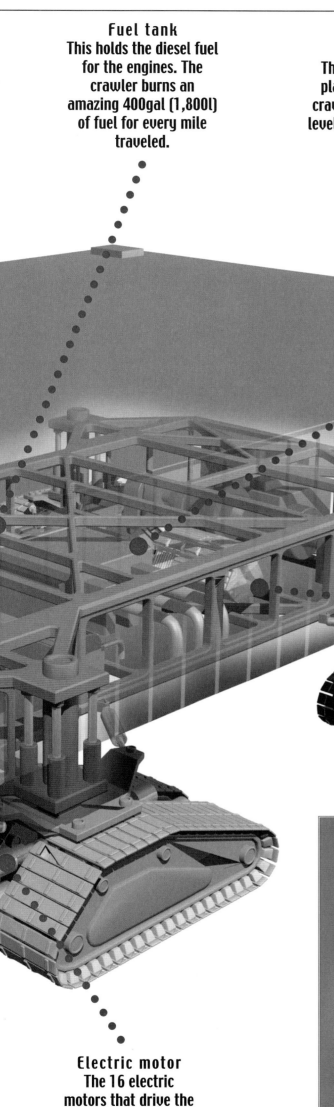

Fuel tank
This holds the diesel fuel for the engines. The crawler burns an amazing 400gal (1,800l) of fuel for every mile traveled.

Platform
The Shuttle stands on the deck, or platform. A leveling system in the crawler keeps the platform perfectly level at all times, otherwise the Space Shuttle would fall over.

Engine control room
An engineer in the control room keeps the two large diesel engines and 16 electric motors running smoothly.

Diesel engine
Two diesel engines drive the generators.

Electric motor
The 16 electric motors that drive the crawler are powered by four generators.

IN SLOW MOTION

The crawler's top speed when loaded is 1mph (1.6kph)—though it can reach twice this speed when unloaded! It takes five hours to carry the Space Shuttle to the launch pad. Even at this slow speed, the crawler has traveled a total distance of 2,500mi (4,000km) over the years. This is about the distance from the Kennedy Space Center in Florida, where the crawler is based, to Los Angeles.

When loaded with the Space Shuttle, the crawler is carrying the largest weight ever moved by a land vehicle. The crawler weighs 2,677 tons when unloaded and 8,034 tons when loaded. Perched on top of the crawler, the Shuttle looks like a candle on a cake.

SPACE STATION

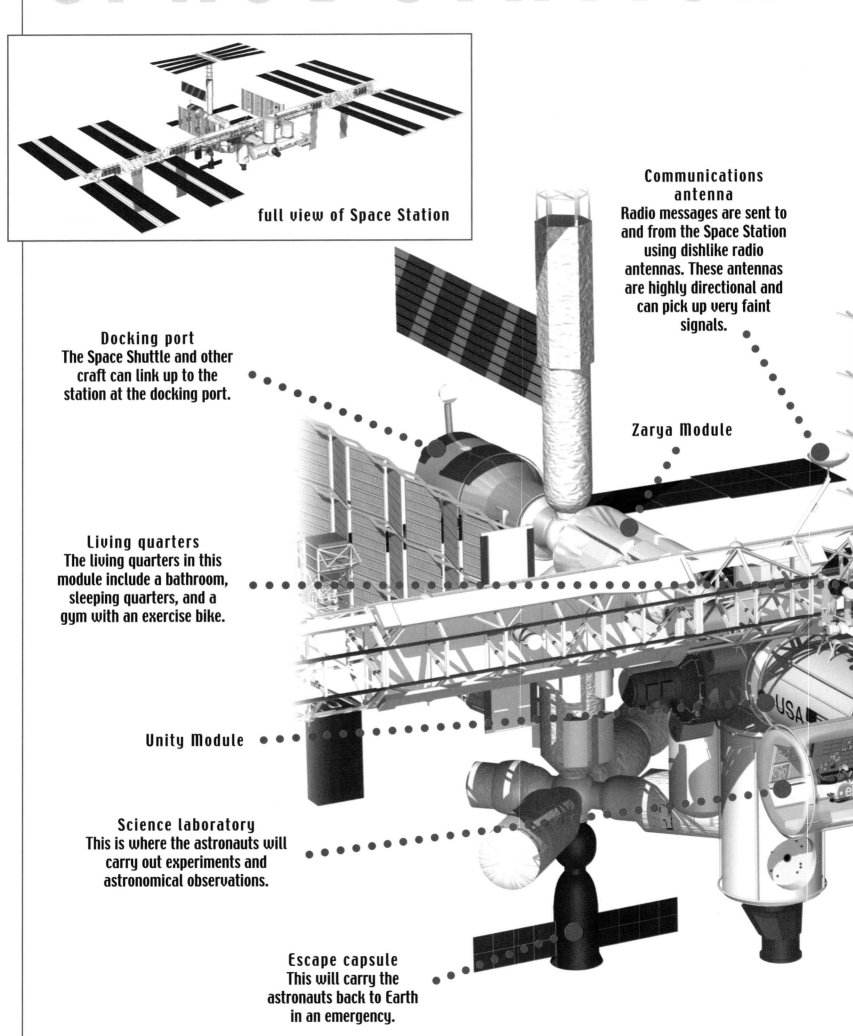

full view of Space Station

Communications antenna
Radio messages are sent to and from the Space Station using dishlike radio antennas. These antennas are highly directional and can pick up very faint signals.

Docking port
The Space Shuttle and other craft can link up to the station at the docking port.

Zarya Module

Living quarters
The living quarters in this module include a bathroom, sleeping quarters, and a gym with an exercise bike.

Unity Module

Science laboratory
This is where the astronauts will carry out experiments and astronomical observations.

Escape capsule
This will carry the astronauts back to Earth in an emergency.

BUILDING THE SPACE STATION

The world's most exciting space project, the International Space Station, is currently being built 217mi (350km) in orbit above the Earth. Assembly of the Space Station began in December 1998 and will be completed in 2004. The Space Station will be a gigantic 354ft (108m) across and 148ft (88m) long. It will weigh over 423 tons. It will take 45 shuttle launches to carry the construction parts of the station into orbit.

NASA will carry out most of the construction work and provide most of the modules that make up the station. Russia, Europe, Japan, Canada, and Brazil will also take part in the building and operation of the station.

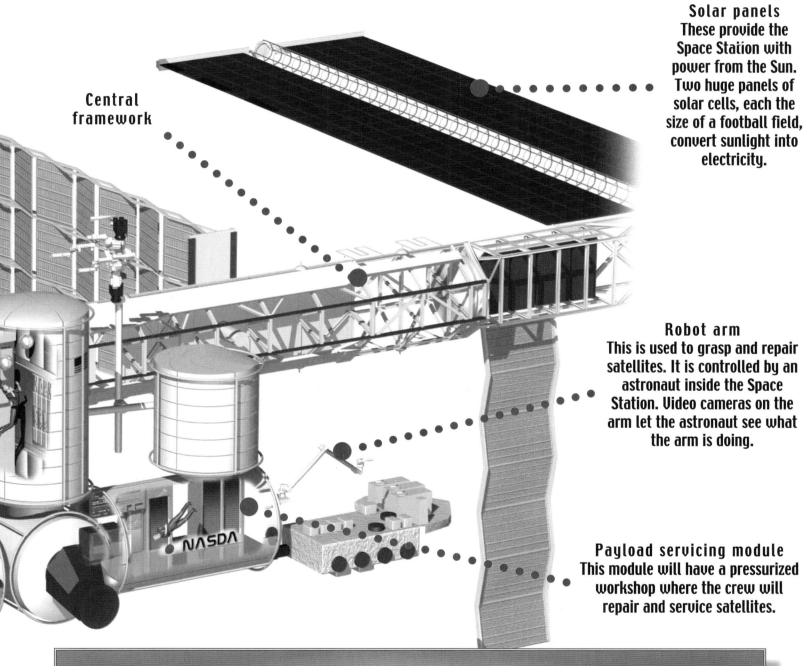

Central framework

Solar panels
These provide the Space Station with power from the Sun. Two huge panels of solar cells, each the size of a football field, convert sunlight into electricity.

Robot arm
This is used to grasp and repair satellites. It is controlled by an astronaut inside the Space Station. Video cameras on the arm let the astronaut see what the arm is doing.

Payload servicing module
This module will have a pressurized workshop where the crew will repair and service satellites.

LIVING AND WORKING IN SPACE

The station will have modules for astronauts to live and work in. The modules will be attached to a long spine of inter-connecting beams called a truss. Huge solar panels will supply the station with electricity.

Up to seven astronauts will spend up to three months at a time working in the station. They will carry out all kinds of experiments and observations in orbit. The almost complete absence of gravity on the Space Station will allow experiments that are impossible on Earth. The station will also be used for recovering and repairing weather and communications satellites.

FUTURE MACHINES

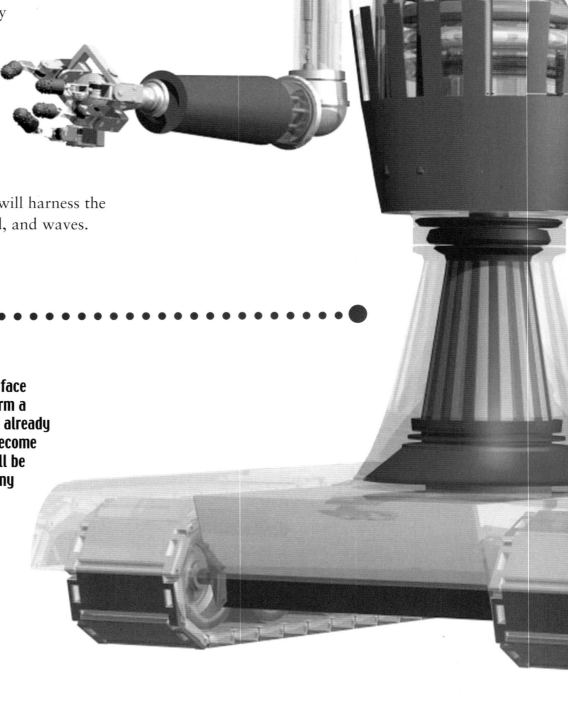

What kind of monster machines will be invented in the future? Today's monster machines do jobs that we can't do ourselves. The machines of the future might help us to solve the problems that we cannot solve ourselves.

ENERGY CRISIS

One big problem we have at the moment is our energy supplies. The Earth's supplies of fossil fuels are being used up fast. Oil will last only another 50 years. Coal will also run out. One of today's monster machines—the nuclear reactor—can make a contribution to our future energy needs. But nuclear power is expensive and creates dangerous waste products.

A new type of nuclear power, called fusion power, is being developed, but this has the same disadvantages. Maybe the power machines of the future will harness the renewable energy of the Sun, wind, and waves.

FUTURE ROBOT
A humanlike appearance is a good idea for household robots, but their friendly face hides a powerful machine able to perform a variety of tasks. Robots like these have already been built, but in the future they will become more useful and more reliable. They will be able to see and speak and carry out many household chores.

THINKING MACHINES

We already have monster machines that can do hard and boring work. In the future, we will need thinking machines that can do complicated jobs on their own. Industrial robots will obey spoken instructions, and even respond to thought control. They will be able to see and to talk. Above all, they will be intelligent.

We already have intelligent computers. They can solve problems and play complicated games like chess. Chess machines can beat almost all human opponents. In the future, their intelligence will be much greater. Intelligent computers will be able to take over much of the brain work done by scientists and others today. Perhaps your teacher will be replaced by a computer. That would definitely be a monster machine! Would you like an intelligent computer that could go to school for you? At school the machine could sit in the classroom and absorb knowledge from the computerized teacher. Each night, while you would sleep, the knowledge could be downloaded into your brain. Each morning you would wake up brainier than you were the previous day!

KEEPING CONTROL

Science fiction stories warn that intelligent machines might eventually take control of the world away from humans. However, machines have always been our helpers and under our control. Humans can control the huge forces generated by the monster machines described in this book. Hopefully, the machines of the future will also be under our control.

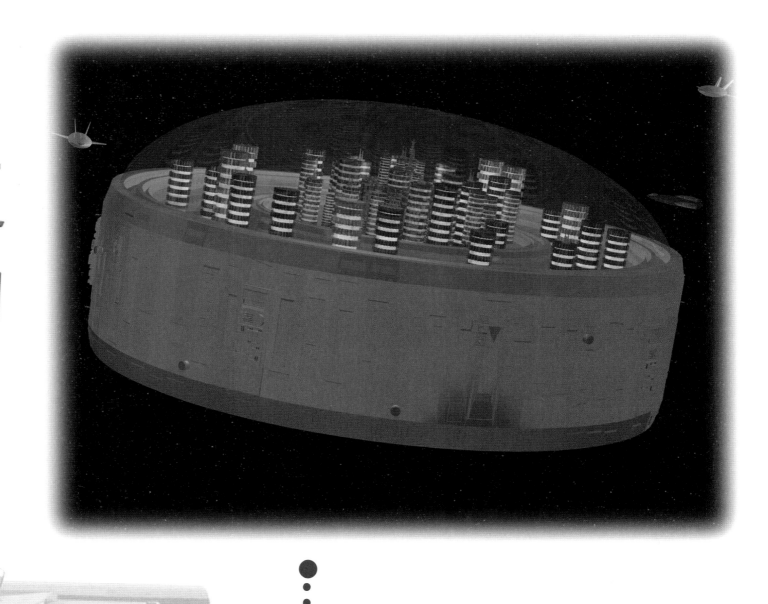

CITY IN SPACE
The ultimate space station would be a city in space, where millions of people could live under a transparent dome. The station would spin slowly to produce artificial gravity, similar to that on Earth. Residents might mainly be astronomers and other scientists working in laboratories beneath the city. The station might also accommodate tourists, but vacations in space will probably always be very expensive.

GLOSSARY

aggregate Broken rock laid as a foundation under a road or railroad track, or used to make concrete.

asphalt A mixture of tar and crushed rock that is spread on the surface of a road.

auger A device used to lift liquid or powder. An auger is a turning spiral inside a tube or cylinder.

ballast Material loaded into the bottom of a ship or oil rig to help keep it steady in stormy weather.

calender The set of rollers that press a sheet of paper to smooth its surface.

centrifugal force The force that throws occupants of a car, for example, to one side when the car goes around a corner.

conveyor belt A continuous belt on which goods or materials are moved.

counterweight A heavy weight attached to a crane or other lifting machine to balance the weight of the object being lifted.

filter A device that removes impurities, such as dust, from the liquid or gas that passes through it.

freight Goods or materials carried by road, rail, or air.

gravity The force that pulls objects toward the Earth and makes them fall.

hopper A funnel-shaped opening or container used to load material into a machine.

hydraulic machine A machine worked by water, oil, or some other liquid.

inertia The tendency that all objects have to remain motionless or moving at a constant speed unless acted upon by a force.

interferometer A type of telescope that combines two small telescopes to produce the effect of a large telescope.

jib The arm of a crane that reaches over the load.

letterpress A type of printing process that uses raised metal letters to print the words onto a page.

lithography A type of printing process that uses a flat printing plate. The letters to be printed are formed on the plate in ink and transferred to paper during printing.

mass dampener A heavy weight sometimes built into a tall building to keep it from swaying in strong winds.

metal ore A rock or mineral from which metal can be extracted.

neutron A small particle found inside atoms.

outrigger Legs or stabilizers that keep a crane or concrete mixer truck steady when the boom or jib is extended.

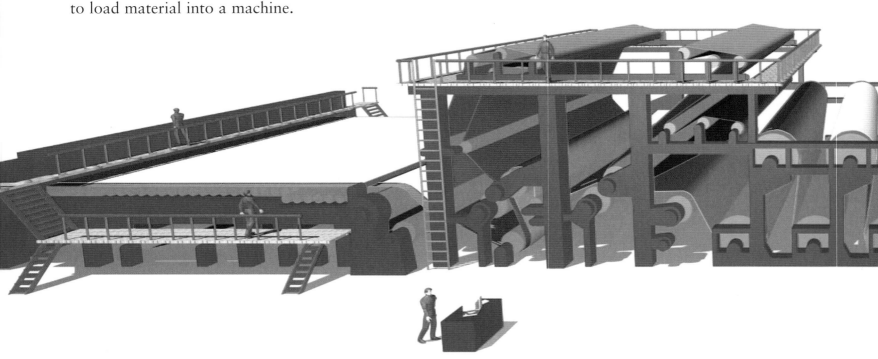

soda A chemical used in glassmaking. Its chemical name is sodium carbonate.

strip mining A method of mining in which the soil overlying a coal or mineral deposit is removed to get at the deposit.

suction pipe A pipe that sucks up liquid or other materials.

turbine A kind of engine that is powered by a jet of gas, such as steam, or liquid such as water.

turbogenerator A machine used to produce electricity in which a turbine operates an electrical generator.

oxidize A chemical process in which a material combines with oxygen.

piston The part of an engine that moves inside the cylinder.

press roller A cylinder in a papermaking machine that squeezes water out of the newly made paper.

pulp A soft, wet mass of material—for example, a pulp of wet newspaper.

silt The mud and small rocks found at the bottom of rivers, canals, and the ocean.

web In printing or papermaking, the long strip of paper being printed or made.

winch A device for lifting things using a rope wound around a cylinder.

INDEX